First Look at...
Quattro Pro 2.0/3.0

Lisa Rosner

Mitchell McGRAW-HILL

New York St. Louis San Francisco Auckland Bogotá Caracas Hamburg
Lisbon London Madrid Mexico Milan Montreal New Delhi Paris
San Juan São Paulo Singapore Sydney Tokyo Toronto Watsonville

Mitchell **McGRAW-HILL**
Watsonville, CA 95076

First Look at Quattro Pro 2.0/3.0

Copyright © 1992 by **McGRAW-HILL, Inc.** All rights reserved. Printed in the United States of America. Except as permitted under the United States Copyright Act of 1976, no part of this publication may be reproduced or distributed in any form or by any means, or stored in a database or retrieval system, without the prior written permission of the publisher.

2 3 4 5 6 7 8 9 0 DOH DOH 9 0 9 8 7 6 5 4 3 2

ISBN 0-07-053811-5

Sponsoring editor: Roger Howell
Editorial assistant: Laurie Boudreau
Director of production: Jane Somers
Production assistant: Leslie Austin
Project manager: Eve Strock, Bookman Productions
Interior designer: Renee Deprey
Cover designer: Janet Bollow
Cover photo: W. Warren/**West**light
Compositor: Brent Jones
Printer and binder: R.R. Donnelley & Sons

Library of Congress Card Catalog No. 91-066892

Quattro Pro is a registered trademark of Borland International, Inc.

Contents

Preface ix

LESSON 1

Exploring Quattro Pro   1

Objectives   1

How to Use This Book   1

What Is Quattro Pro?   1

Special Keys   2

Starting Quattro Pro   2

The Spreadsheet   4

    Moving Around the Spreadsheet • Editing Cell Information •
Labels, Values, and Formulas • Shortcut for Entering Data •
Formulas Using Cell Addesses • Deleting Cell Contents

Command Menu   7

    Choosing a Command • Menu Terminology

Saving Your Spreadsheet   9

Exiting Quattro Pro   10

Summary of Commands   11

Self-Test   11

LESSON 2

Creating a Spreadsheet Application   13

Objectives   13

Creating a Spreadsheet   13

Making Use of Formulas   15

Relative and Absolute Cell Addresses   16

Using a Cell Address in a Formula Without Typing   17

Adding Columns   18

Using Functions Without Typing   19

iii

iv Contents

Changing the Way Values Are Displayed   20
Changing Column Width   22
Shortcut Key for Saving Files   23
Shortcut Key for Exiting Quattro Pro   24
Summary of Commands   24
Self-Test   24

LESSON 3   Editing a Spreadsheet   26

Objectives   26
Opening a Spreadsheet   26
Changing Values in a Spreadsheet   27
Inserting and Deleting Rows and Columns   28
    Inserting Rows • Inserting Columns • Deleting Columns
Subtotals: More About Formulas   31
Copying Cells   32
    Copying and Modifying Labels • Copying Numbers •
    Copying Formulas and Functions with Cell Addresses
Moving the Contents of a Cell   34
Saving a File after Modifying It   35
Summary of Commands   36
Self-Test   36

LESSON 4   Advanced Editing Techniques   38

Objectives   38
Extended Mode   40
Lines and Boxes   42
    Deleting Lines and Boxes
Printing a Section of a Spreadsheet   46
Deleting a Section of a Spreadsheet   46
Summary of Commands   47
Self-Test   48

LESSON 5   More About Functions   49

Objectives   49
Changing Alignment   51

Contents **v**

Combining Currency and Comma (Financial) Format in a Column 51

Using @COUNT, @MAX, and @MIN functions 52

Using the @PMT Function 54

Creating Links Between Different Parts of the Spreadsheet 55

Copying Functions 56

Solve For 58

Using the @IF Function 61

Summary of Commands 62

Self-Test 63

LESSON 6 Setting Up a Database **65**

Objectives 65

Designing a Database 65

Filling a Block with Sequential Values 68

Assigning Names to Fields 69

Sorting the Database 70

Searching Through Your Data 72

Extracting Records from a Database 73

Summary of Commands 75

Self-Test 75

LESSON 7 Creating Graphs **77**

Objectives 77

Creating a Graph 77

Graph Type 78

Series 78

Displaying the Graph 80

Editing Series 82

Adding Text 82

Saving a Graph 84

Displaying a Named Graph 84

Closing a Spreadsheet 85

Adding Interior Labels 87

Editing Labels

Adding a Second Line to the Title 89

vi Contents

Summary of Commands   90
Self-Test   90

LESSON 8   Annotating Graphs   92

Objectives   92
Creating a Pie Graph   92
Reasons for Annotating a Graph   93
Retrieving a File   94
Graph Reset   94
Removing Grid Lines   97
Annotating a Graph   97
Creating a Text Box   99
Drawing Arrows   100
Quitting the Annotator   101
Saving Changes to a Graph   102
Summary of Commands   102
Self-Test   103

LESSON 9   Linking Spreadsheets   105

Objectives   105
Opening and Displaying More Than One Spreadsheet   107
   Moving Within Windows • Zooming In to a Window •
   Moving Between Windows
Creating Links in Formulas   109
Changing Linked References   111
   Creating Links in Functions
@IF Function   112
Hiding Columns   113
Summary of Commands   115
Self-Test   116

LESSON 10   Printing Spreadsheets and Graphs   117

Objectives   117
Inserting Page Breaks   117
Setting Headers and Footers   118

Contents **vii**

Using Screen Preview 119

Printing a Spreadsheet Report 121
Interrupting Printing • Saving Print Settings

Dividing Wide Spreadsheets into Pages 122

Retrieving a Linked Spreadsheet 122

Setting Margins 123

Creating Headings from Row and Column Labels 124

Setting Up a Graph to Print 125
Graph Layout Settings • Previewing a Graph • Printing a Graph

Summary of Commands 128

Self-Test 130

Using a Mouse with Quattro Pro **131**

Self-Test Answers **133**

Quattro Pro 2.0/3.0 Command Summary **136**

Index **145**

Preface

First Look at Quattro Pro 2.0/3.0 is a step-by-step, hands-on tutorial covering Quattro Pro's introductory and intermediate features. You can use this book as a self-paced guide, in a lecture class that teaches the basics of Quattro Pro, or as a supplememental text in a variety of classes.

First Look at Quattro Pro 2.0/3.0 will quickly get you "up to speed" with the program's most useful features. Complete with a comprehensive command summary at the end of the book, *First Look at Quattro Pro 2.0/3.0* makes reference quick and easy.

ORGANIZATION

Each lesson contains the following features:

- A list of objectives followed by an overview of the lesson
- A hands-on tutorial that guides you through specific functions and commands
- Caution and Note sections that appear throughout the lesson, alerting you to common program pitfalls
- A summary of commands that includes the page number where each command was first introduced
- A self-test that reinforces learning

As you work through *First Look at Quattro Pro 2.0/3.0*, you will create files that are used again in later lessons. You should save these files on your own data diskette so you can locate and retrieve them easily.

The commands and features discussed in this book will work with either version 2.0 or 3.0 of Quattro Pro. However, if your computer is set up in version 3.0 in WYSIWYG (what you see is what you get) mode, the appearance of Quattro Pro menus and spreadsheets will differ slightly from the illustrations in the text.

x   Preface

FIRST LOOK AT... SERIES

This book is part of the First Look at... series, which consists of titles designed to cover the most popular commercial software packages.

The purpose of each book in this series is to provide an inexpensive, quick, and complete learning tool that you can use for ready reference after you've completed the tutorial. At the end of each book, a comprehensive summary of commands, arranged alphabetically, makes reference easy. It is assumed that you have access to the complete software package and all its features.

In a minimum number of pages, each book covers the most commonly used features of the particular program—enough to equip students with fundamental proficiency in a short time.

ACKNOWLEDGMENTS

The Humanities Computer Lab and my students in the Historical Studies Program at Stockton State College provided the opportunity and inspiration that led to this book. I would also like to thank John Theibault, Henry Rosner, Lillian Rosner, Mark Rosner, and Andrew Rosner for their invaluable help and encouragement throughout the project. Larry D. Scott, of Ricks College, reviewed the text and offered excellent suggestions.

Lisa Rosner
Stockton State College
Pomona, New Jersey

 # Exploring Quattro Pro

OBJECTIVES

At the end of this lesson, you will be able to:

- Use the keyboard.
- Start Quattro Pro.
- Recognize the parts of a spreadsheet.
- Move around the spreadsheet.
- Enter values, labels, and formulas into cells.
- Edit and delete cell contents.
- Activate the command menu.
- Open and close a pull-down menu.
- Save a spreadsheet.
- Exit Quattro Pro.

HOW TO USE THIS BOOK

This book assumes that you are using Quattro Pro, version 2.0 or 3.0. The book is organized into 10 lessons, each covering a separate topic. Later lessons build on skills acquired in earlier ones, so it is recommended that you do each lesson in order. The book also assumes that you begin each lesson by starting Quattro Pro and end each lesson by saving your work and exiting Quattro Pro.

WHAT IS QUATTRO PRO?

Quattro Pro is a powerful electronic spreadsheet. A **spreadsheet** is a program used for all kinds of mathematical calculations and data analysis. It can make the simplest addition and subtraction easier; it can also be used for sophisti-

2　First Look at Quattro Pro 2.0/3.0

cated market research and analysis. This book is designed to teach you the basic skills you will need to use Quattro Pro on your own and to introduce you to its most important features. It is organized around a series of hands-on applications, each designed to emphasize a different set of features. Each lesson ends with a self-test at the back, so you can check your newly acquired skills. The best way to check them, however, is to apply them to your own projects. As you go through the book, try to think of how you can use your growing knowledge of spreadsheets in your own work or class.

SPECIAL KEYS

If you haven't used a computer before, take time to examine the keyboard. Most keys are exactly like typewriter keys, and you type on them as you would on a typewriter. Instead of appearing on paper, though, the words you type appear on the computer monitor.

The keyboard also contains some special keys used only in computer programs: [Enter] (also called [Return] in some programs), the function keys ([F1], [F2], [F3], [F4], [F5], [F6], [F7], [F8], [F9], [F10]), and the arrow keys ([←], [→], [↑], and [↓]). Other special keys are [Ctrl], [Esc], [Ins], and [Alt], [Del] and [Backspace], and [Home], [End], [Pg Up], and [Pg Dn]. A familiar key with a special use in Quattro Pro is the [/].

For most keystrokes, you press the key for the count of 1, as you would on a typewriter. For some commands, though, Quattro Pro expects you to press one key while holding down another. In this book, such commands are written as two keys separated by a hyphen. For example, the shortcut for the Save command, [Ctrl]-[S] (discussed in Lesson Two), requires you to press both [Ctrl] and [S]. To get the feel of doing this, think of counting 1...2...3. On the count of 1, hold down [Ctrl], on the count of 2, press [S], and on the count of 3 release both keys. You may also be prompted to hold down [Alt] or [Shift] followed by another key. Use whatever fingers you find most comfortable to press special keys.

STARTING QUATTRO PRO

Follow these steps to start Quattro Pro.

1. Turn on the computer. There is one switch on the processing unit (the large box underneath or next to the monitor), and there may be another on the monitor.

Lesson 1/ Exploring Quattro Pro

2. You will see one of two things on the screen:
   (a) A list of choices, called a **menu**. The menu contains instructions; generally you are expected to first press a number or letter corresponding to the program you wish to use and then press [Enter]. Follow the instructions for choosing Quattro Pro.
   (b) A symbol on the screen, which may look like this: "C:\." If you see this symbol, first check with your instructor to find out in what section of the computer, called a **subdirectory**, Quattro Pro is located in. Then, type **cd**\[name of subdirectory].

   For example, if Quattro Pro is located in the subdirectory QPRO, type **cd\qpro** (you can use upper- or lowercase). Then, type **q**.

3. Whichever directions you follow, after a few seconds you should see the opening screen for Quattro Pro (Figure 1-1).

Figure 1-1
Parts of a spreadsheet

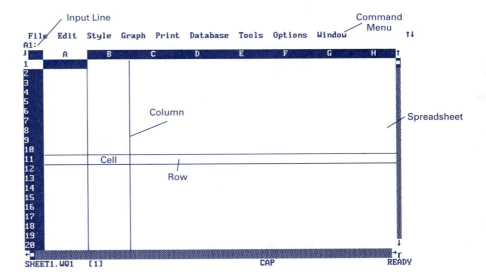

This screen may look like one continuous surface, but it is actually made up of two parts, the **spreadsheet** and the **command menu**. When you first start Quattro Pro, the screen is set up for you to begin typing into a blank spreadsheet. The blank spreadsheet is always initially called SHEET1.WQ1; you can see the name in the lower left corner. You will learn how to change the name at the end of this lesson.

Quattro Pro starts this way because it tries wherever possible to simulate your ordinary working environment. For example, if you were preparing a financial statement by hand rather than on the computer, you would probably start by writing information on a blank sheet of paper. As you worked, you would reach for tools: a ruler, say, a calculator, or scissors and tape.

4 First Look at Quattro Pro 2.0/3.0

Quattro Pro assumes, therefore, that you would prefer to start off by typing information into the spreadsheet, reaching for various tools accessible from the command menu as necessary.

THE SPREADSHEET

All spreadsheets are arranged in **rows** and **columns**. The rows are numbered consecutively, starting with 1 at the upper left corner; the columns are given letters, beginning with A at the upper left corner. The rectangular intersections of rows and columns are called **cells**. Each cell has a unique **cell address**, such as A1, D7, or H15, based on the column and row it is in.

When you start Quattro Pro, you are automatically positioned at cell A1. Type **My First Spreadsheet**.

Notice that the words appear on a line in the upper left corner just under the command menu. That line is the **input line**. If you make a mistake while typing, use the arrow keys to move the cursor and [Del] and [Backspace] to make corrections. The A1 cell stays highlighted, telling you where the words on the input line will eventually go. On the lower right corner you see the word "Label," letting you know that Quattro Pro assumes you are typing a **label**, a set of alphanumeric characters. Press [Enter].

Now the words appear in the spreadsheet. In the input line, you see "A1: 'My First Spreadsheet." A1 is the cell address. The ' indicates that the words will be a left-justified label. "My First Spreadsheet" is what you typed. Labels can also be right-justified or centered; you will find out more about that in Lesson Five.

Moving Around the Spreadsheet

You can move around the spreadsheet in a number of different ways.

1. The arrow keys move one cell in the direction indicated by the keys.

2. [Pg Dn] moves one screen (20 rows) down.

3. [Pg Up] moves one screen (20 rows) up.

4. [Ctrl]-[→] (while holding down [Ctrl], press [→]) moves one screen (8 columns, 9 characters wide) to the right.

5. [Ctrl]-[←] (while holding down [Ctrl], press [←]) moves one screen (8 columns, 9 characters wide) to the left.

6. [F5] is the Go To key. If you press [F5], you will see on the input line: "Enter address to go to:". (The current cell address will be highlighted.)

You can type in whatever cell address you want to go to and press [Enter]. For example, if you are at A1 and want to move to cell G6,

   (a) Press [F5]

   The input line will read "Enter address to go to: A1".

   (b) Type **G6**

   The highlight will appear on G6, and the input line will read "G6," indicating that cell G6 is where new information will go.

7. [Home] returns the cursor to A1. This is especially useful in large spreadsheets.

Take time to practice moving around the spreadsheet.

Editing Cell Information

Press [Home] to return to A1 if you have not already done so. You will see, once again, "A1: 'My First Spreadsheet" in the input line.

Suppose you want to change the title to "My First Quattro Pro Spreadsheet". You could retype the whole label and press [Enter]. (Try it.) The new cell contents will completely erase the old.

An easier method of changing cell contents when you want to edit them, rather than change them completely, is to make sure the cell is highlighted and press [F2]. This will put you in **Edit** mode; you will see the word "Edit" in the lower right corner of the screen to remind you. While in Edit mode, you can use ordinary typing keys, arrow keys, [Backspace] and [Del] to edit cell contents. Edit the label to read "My First Quattro Pro Spreadsheet". Press [Enter] to preerve the changes.

Suppose you've made changes to a cell but decide before you press [Enter] that you don't like them and want to return to the original contents. Just press [Esc].

> *CAUTION: Pressing* [Esc] *will work only if you have not yet pressed* [Enter]. *Once changes are entered, you cannot escape from them by using* [Esc].

Labels, Values, and Formulas

You already know how to enter labels. Quattro Pro calls any word a label since that is how words usually function in a spreadsheet.

Entering **values** is just as easy. Quattro Pro calls any number or any expression that can represent a number a value. For example, 5 is a value, and so is

6 First Look at Quattro Pro 2.0/3.0

5 + 5. Move to A3 and type **2**. The input line says "A3: 2", and in the lower right corner you see the word "Value". Press Enter; A3 now contains the value 2.

Shortcut for Entering Data

You don't have to press Enter every time you enter information. If you press any of the arrow keys to move out of the cell, the information will automatically be entered. Enter the following values in the following cells, using the arrow keys to enter the information and move around the spreadsheet:

1. Move to A4. Type **2** and press →
2. Move to B3. Type **576984** and press ↓
3. At B4, type **4698** and press ←, then ↓

   You should be at A5.

You can see from what you've entered that numbers are automatically right-justified, so they can be presented in an easy-to-read column.

Formulas are also easy. At A5, type **2+2** Enter. In the cell, you will see the correct answer, 4. On the input line, you will see what you actually typed, 2+2. The **input line** shows you the "raw version" of cell contents, which includes both what you type and the additional information that Quattro Pro adds, such as the ' to indicate left alignment for labels. The *cell* shows you the "processed version," the calculated formula or the left-aligned label.

Formulas Using Cell Addresses

Formulas don't have to use numbers. Instead, they can use addresses of the cells containing numbers. (This makes sense. Why would anyone design a computer program where you had to first type numbers into cells and then retype the numbers into formulas?)

To try this, move to A6 and type **+A3+A4** Enter. (You can use uppercase or lowercase letters in formulas.)

The cell again shows the correct answer—still 4—and the input line shows the formula you used to arrive at that answer. But why, you may ask, do you need that first +? Why not just type **A3+A4** Enter? (Try it and see.)

Quattro Pro has assumed that you wanted to type a label and added ' to your formula. You need to type + at the start of any formula where the first item is not a number. The + acts as a signal to Quattro Pro that you are typing a formula, not a label. The basic arithmetic symbols you can use in a formula are:

+   plus

−   minus

Lesson 1/ Exploring Quattro Pro **7**

*	multiplied by
/	divided by
<	less than
>	greater than
=	equal to
<>	not equal to

In a formula containing several operations, Quattro Pro multiplies and divides numbers first and then adds and subtracts. For example, in the equation 5+6*17+24, Quattro Pro first multiplies 6*17, and then adds 5 and 24. In the equation A3+A4*B3, Quattro Pro first multiplies A4*B3, and then adds A3. To change the order of operation, you can group expressions by using parentheses: (5+6)*(17+24) or +(A3+A4)*B3.

Deleting Cell Contents

To delete cell contents, position the highlight on the cell and press Del. Move to A5. Press Del. The formula is deleted.

. . . .
COMMAND MENU

By now, you should be comfortable with the spreadsheet. It is time to turn your attention to the **menu** at the top of the screen.

Choosing a Command

To choose a command, you have to "jump" out of the spreadsheet to the menu. You cannot do this by just pressing ↑ or Pg Up (try it). Instead, you must press /. Once you press /, you will notice that the word "File" in the menu is highlighted, and the word "Menu" appears in the lower right corner. On the bottom left, you will see a brief description of the menu choice, in this case reading File Operations. This type of menu is called a **pull-down menu** (see Figure 1-2). The words at the top of the screen give you the general categories of commands. For a specific command, you must "pull down" the list of commands. To do this, you can either

- Use the arrow keys to move around the menu until the category you want is highlighted and then press Enter,

    or

- Just press the highlighted letter on the choice you want.

Figure 1-2
Pull–down menu

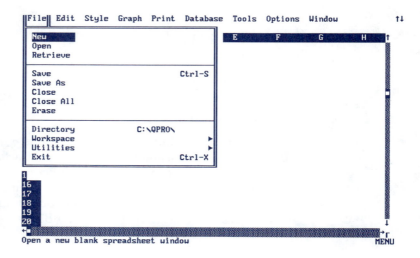

For example, to pull down the file operations menu, you could either

- Make sure the word File is highlighted, and press [Enter],

  or

- Just press [F].

Either way, you will see a screen resembling Figure 1-2. To close up any menu you've pulled down, press [Esc].

Press [/]. Practice using arrow keys to move around the command menu and pulling down different menus. As you highlight each choice, a brief description appears in the bottom left corner. Notice too that next to their names, some choices have Ctrl and a letter, such as Ctrl-S. These are the shortcut keys you can use for the most frequently used commands. Don't worry about them right now; we'll use them in the next lesson.

To jump from the command menu back to the spreadsheet, press [Esc]. You will become very familiar with using [/] and [Esc] to move back and forth between the spreadsheet and menu in Quattro Pro. Press [Esc].

Menu Terminology

When this book requires you to choose a menu item, the following instructions will appear: "/ [**M**ain menu choice] ¦[**S**ubmenu choice]," which means, "Press [/], then the highlighted letter for the main menu item, and then the highlighted letter for the submenu item." For example, "/File¦Save" means "Press [/], then [F], then [S]."

Go on to the next section for an example of this.

Lesson 1/ Exploring Quattro Pro   9

SAVING YOUR SPREADSHEET

> **CAUTION:** Always save your spreadsheet before leaving Quattro Pro and turning off the computer. Otherwise all your hard work will be lost!

To save your spreadsheet with the name FIRST.WQ1, select **/File¦Save**.

1. Press `/` (to activate the menu)
2. Press `F` (to choose **F**ile Operations).
3. Press `S` (for **S**ave).

You could also have pressed `↓` until Save was highlighted and pressed `Enter`. Your screen will resemble Figure 1-3 (the list of files may be slightly different).

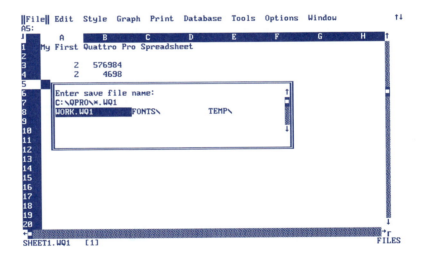

Figure 1-3
Saving a file

If the prompt begins with the disk drive and directory you want to save the file to, just type the name you want the file to have and press `Enter`. Quattro Pro will automatically add the suffix .WQ1. That is, if the prompt begins with the disk drive C and the directory \QPRO, as in Figure 1-3, and you want to save the file to C:\QPRO, just type the filename. If the prompt begins A:\ and you want to save the file to a floppy disk in the A drive, first make sure there is a disk in the drive and then type the filename. When you press `Enter`, the file will be saved to the specified disk and directory. If you wish to save the file to a disk drive other than the one in the prompt, press `Esc` until the prompt is cleared and then type the disk drive followed by the filename. That is, if the prompt is C:\QPRO and you wish to save the file to a floppy disk in the A drive, first press [Esc] twice to clear the prompt and then type **A:FIRST** and press [Enter].

The following steps assume you do not want to change the disk drive or directory:

1. Type **First**

   (You can type upper- or lowercase letters.)

2. Press [Enter]

   Your file will be saved with the name FIRST.WQ1.

EXITING QUATTRO PRO

To leave Quattro Pro, choose **/File |Exit** from the menu, Press [/], then [F], then [X]. Notice that the *x*, not the *E*, is highlighted in Exit.

If you have just saved your spreadsheet, you will be returned to where you started when you first turned on the computer, either the original menu or the C:\ prompt. If you have not yet saved your spreadsheet or if you made changes in it after saving it, your screen will resemble Figure 1-4. This is

Figure 1-4
Exiting Quattro Pro

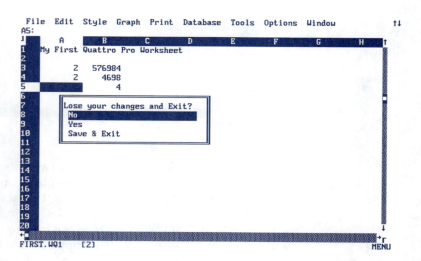

another kind of menu, called a **pop-up menu**, because it pops up only under certain circumstances, such as when you try to leave Quattro Pro without saving your work. It operates in the same way as the command menu: You

Lesson 1/ Exploring Quattro Pro   **11**

can either use the arrow keys to move among the choices and press Enter when the proper choice is highlighted, or you can press the highlighted key in the choice you want.

To save your work, choose Save and Exit, and follow the instructions in the last section for saving your spreadsheet.

When you see the original menu or prompt, you can turn off the computer.

■ SUMMARY OF COMMANDS

Topic or Feature	Command or Reference	Menu	Page
Activate Command Menu	/		7
Begin a Formula with a Cell Address	+		6
Cancel an Action	Esc		5
Delete Cell Contents	Del		7
Edit a Cell	F2		5
Enter Data	Enter or highlight movement keys		6
Exit Quattro Pro	Exit	/File ¦Exit	10
Go To a Specific Cell	F5		4
Leave Command Menu	Esc		8
Load Quattro Pro	Q, from Quattro Pro subdirectory		
Move Left One Screen	Ctrl-←		4
Move Right One Screen	Ctrl-→		4
Move Down One Screen	Pg Dn		4
Move Up One Screen	Pg Up		4
Save a Spreadsheet	Save	/File ¦Save	9
Select Command on Menu Bar	/, letter		8

■ SELF-TEST

1. What are the two parts of the initial Quattro Pro screen?_____

_____

12 First Look at Quattro Pro 2.0/3.0

2. What name does Quattro Pro give the initial blank spreadsheet? _____

_____ .

3. How are columns designated in a spreadsheet? _____

_____ .

4. How are rows designated in a spreadsheet? _____

_____ .

5. What is a cell in Quattro Pro? _____

_____ .

6. How does a cell get a cell address? _____

_____ .

7. Explain what pressing the following keys will do:
Pg Up , Pg Dn , Ctrl -→ , Ctrl -← , F5 , Home

_____

_____ .

8. Pressing _____ allows you to edit cell contents.

9. What is the difference between a label and a value? _____

_____ .

10. How do you delete the contents of a cell? _____

_____ .

11. Pressing _____ activates the command menu.

12. How do you pull down a particular menu? _____

_____ .

13. What two methods can you use to choose a command or feature from a
menu? _____ .

14. Press _____ to close up a menu.

15. Press _____ to jump back from the command menu to the spreadsheet.

Creating a Spreadsheet Application

OBJECTIVES

At the end of this lesson, you will be able to:

- Create a spreadsheet by entering labels, values, and formulas.
- Enter cell addresses in formulas without typing them out.
- Recognize absolute and relative cell addresses.
- Insert absolute cell addresses into formulas without typing.
- Use the @SUM function to add up cells.
- Use the function menu to enter functions without typing.
- Display values in currency format.
- Change the width of columns.
- Use shortcut keys to save spreadsheets.
- Use shortcut keys to exit Quattro Pro.

CREATING A SPREADSHEET

As you learned in Lesson One, you create a spreadsheet by entering information into the blank spreadsheet you see when you start Quattro Pro. To see what you can do with the spreadsheet, imagine that you have been on a number of business trips lately. You made two trips within the United States, to Seattle and New York; you also traveled to Montreal and Paris. Now you want to document your expenses, either for work or for the Internal Revenue Service. You kept your receipts, so you could add them up with a calculator. But some receipts are in foreign currency, so you have to change them into U.S. dollars. Besides, wouldn't it be nice to have subtotals for each trip and keep the information in a permanent record that you could print out for your files? Using a spreadsheet makes these tasks much easier.

To find out how, start Quattro Pro and, when you see the blank spreadsheet, type the title "Travel Expenses". At A1, type **Travel Expenses** and press Enter.

Then press F5 (the Go To key, remember?) to move to B3, and enter the

13

14 First Look at Quattro Pro 2.0/3.0

information in the following list. Start with Seattle in B3, and enter the names of the cities in column B, the type of expenses in column C, the amounts in column D, and the type of currency in column E. You can enter it in whatever order is easiest for you.

	A	B	C	D	E
3		Seattle	Hotel	300	
4			Meals	150	
5			Airfare	735	
6			Taxi	50	
7		New York	Hotel	500	
8			Meals	250	
9			Airfare	400	
10			Taxi	75	
11		Montreal	Hotel	250	Canadian
12			Meals	175	Canadian
13			Airfare	568	
14			Taxi	35	Canadian
15		Paris	Hotel	2000	Fr
16			Meals	1570	Fr
17			Airfare	898	
18			Taxi	340	Fr
19		Total Expenses:			

Be careful to put the labels Canadian and Fr in column E instead of including them in column D. Column D must have only numbers for Quattro Pro to add them correctly. Total expenses should be in column B19. When you are done, it should look like Figure 2-1.

Figure 2-1
Travel expenses spreadsheet

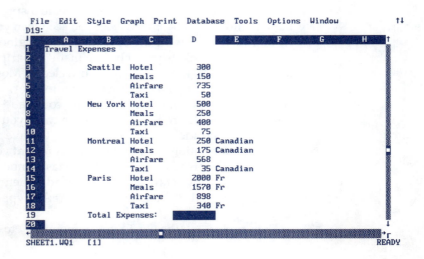

Lesson 2/ Creating a Spreadsheet Application   **15**

MAKING USE OF FORMULAS

What you would like to do is add the expenses and put the total in cell D19. As the list stands now, though, you can't, because some of the values are in foreign currency.

One way to change that is to use simple formulas. For example, $1 Canadian is equal to $0.87 U.S. You can therefore multiply the values in Canadian dollars by .87 to get U.S. dollars. Try this for the hotel bill from Montreal:

1. Move to cell D11 (use [F5]).

2. Press [F2]

3. Edit the value to read "**250∗.87**".

4. Press [Enter]

   D11 should now say "217.5". The input line will tell you the formula you used, "250∗.87", to get that result. Since that value is in U.S. currency, you no longer need the Canadian label. Delete it by moving to cell E11 and pressing [Del].

> **CAUTION: Always remember to modify your labels as appropriate when working on a spreadsheet. Otherwise you may lose track of what your values refer to.**

Using formulas with values will give the correct answer, but by using formulas you have to retype the exchange rate each time. Wouldn't it be easier to just enter the exchange rate once and refer to it whenever you want to use it? Thanks to the spreadsheet formulas you learned in Lesson One, that's precisely what you can do.

1. Move to F3 (use [F5]).

2. Type **Canadian**=[→]

3. Type **.87** [↓][←]

4. Type **Fr**=[→]

5. Type **.17** and press [Enter]

Make sure that column F contains the labels and column G contains only numbers.

Move back to D11 (use [F5]). Press [F2] to edit the formula.

16 First Look at Quattro Pro 2.0/3.0

> **CAUTION: Always remember to press** F2 **if you wish to change information you've already entered into a cell rather than completely erase it. If you move to a cell and start typing without pressing** F2 **, you'll lose the existing cell contents. If you notice that you've done this before pressing** Enter **, you can get the original contents back by pressing** Esc **.**

In the formula, you will insert the cell address G3 in place of .87. Before you type anything, though, we need to explain the difference between relative and absolute cell addresses.

RELATIVE AND ABSOLUTE CELL ADDRESSES

In Lesson One, you learned that you can type in a cell address—G3, for example—instead of a number in a formula. When a cell address in a formula is written G3, it is called a **relative cell address** because it tells Quattro Pro to locate the cell by its position *relative* to the formula. In this case, if a formula in cell D11 includes the relative cell address G3, it tells Quattro Pro to look for the cell three columns to the right and eight rows up.

This is fine as long as you don't plan to reorganize the spreadsheet. But what if you sort the rows in a different order? The formula in D11 might end up in a different cell, but Quattro Pro would still expect the formula to refer to a cell three columns to the right and eight rows up. (We discuss sorting in a later lesson.) That assumption would result in an incorrect answer.

The way to get around this problem is to use an **absolute cell address** by inserting $ before each part of the cell address, like this: G3. That way, even if the row containing the formula is sorted, Quattro Pro will always look in cell G3 for the value to use.

But, you may be thinking, isn't it a bother to type all those $s? Yes, it would be—if you had to do it. Fortunately, Quattro Pro provides a shortcut for you, the key F4 . This shortcut is best illustrated by returning to the Travel Expenses spreadsheet. You should be at cell D11.

1. Press F2 , and edit the formula by deleting .87, if you have not already done so.

2. Press Enter to preserve the change.

Lesson 2/ Creating a Spreadsheet Application **17**

. . . .
USING A CELL ADDRESS IN A FORMULA WITHOUT TYPING

To insert a *relative cell address* in a formula,

1. First, make sure you have reached the point in the formula where you would ordinarily type in the cell address.

   In this case, the input line should read "D11: 250*".

2. Now, press ⬆ and ➡ until cell G3 is highlighted. (You can't use F5 this time.) As you move through the spreadsheet, you'll notice that the input line keeps changing with every cell you pass through.

   When you reach G3, the input line should read: "D11: 250*G3".

3. Press Enter to enter the formula. This calculates the value and returns you to D11.

   The input line stays the same, but the cell reads "217.5".

That was for practice. In this case, what we really want to use is the absolute cell address. The procedure for an absolute cell address is very similar. To insert an *absolute cell address* in a formula,

1. At D11, press F2 , and edit the value by deleting G3.

2. Again, make sure you have reached the point in the formula where you would ordinarily type in the cell address. In this case, the input line should read:"D11: 250*".

3. Press ⬆ and ➡ to move to cell G3.

   When you reach G3, the input line will read: "D11: 250*G3".

4. This time, you want to add $s to the cell address, so press F4

   The input line should now read: "D11: 250*G3".

5. Now, press Enter to enter the formula. This calculates the value and returns you to D11.

   The input line stays the same, and the cell reads "217.5".

Follow the same procedure to convert the rest of the values in Canadian dollars to U.S. dollars. Then, edit cells D15, D16, and D18 to achieve the same result for the values in French currency. One French franc is equal to $0.17 U.S., so you must multiply the values in French currency by .17, the value you entered in G4, to get U.S. dollars. Don't forget to delete the labels Canadian and Fr once you have converted all the values to U.S. currency.

When you are done, the spreadsheet should look like Figure 2-2.

18 First Look at Quattro Pro 2.0/3.0

Figure 2-2
All expenses converted to U.S. dollars

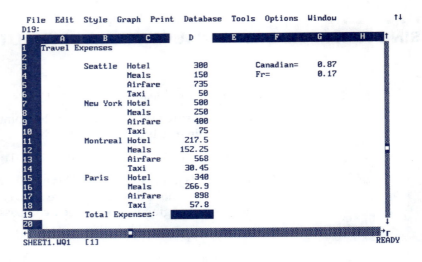

ADDING COLUMNS

Now that you have entered your data and converted all the currency to U.S. dollars, you are ready to add the figures to get your total expenses. You already know one way to add all the expenses: You can move to D19 and type the formula

+D3+D4+D5+D6+D7+D8+D9+D10+D11+D12+D13+D14+D15+D16+D17+D18

That is a lot of work, though, and Quattro Pro always tries to save you work, which is why Quattro Pro has built-in formulas, called **functions**, for many common mathematical tasks, including this one.

Functions are always preceded by the symbol @ and always include cell addresses in parentheses. You can see a pop-up menu with a complete list of all Quattro Pro functions by pressing (Alt)-(F3) (while holding down the (Alt) key, press (F3)). Use (Pg Dn), (Pg Up), (↑), and (↓) to move through the list. When done, press (Esc) to remove the pop-up menu from the screen.

The function you want to use to add the values in column D is @SUM. You want to sum all the values in cells D3 through D18, inclusive. To enter this in cell D19, you type **@SUM(D3..D18)**

@SUM( ) is the function.

D3 is the starting cell.

.. is the pointer. It means "use all cells from the starting cell to the ending cell inclusive."

D18 is the ending cell.

Lesson 2/ Creating a Spreadsheet Application   **19**

Put together, D3..D18 is called a **block** because it refers to a block of cells, as you will see in the next section.

Move to D19, if you are not there already, and type **@SUM(D3..D18)**. Press Enter. You should see the correct answer, 4990.9, in D19.

USING FUNCTIONS WITHOUT TYPING

Typing functions, like typing formulas with cell addresses, can be tedious and can cause mistakes. Quattro Pro therefore gives you ways to enter functions without typing them out. Follow these six steps to enter the @SUM function without typing.

1. First, make sure the cell address where you want to place the function is highlighted. In this case, D19 should be highlighted.

2. Next, press Alt-F3 to bring up the list of functions. The list is alphabetical. Use Pg Dn and ↓ to move to the function you wish to use. This time, when you get to SUM, press Enter.

3. The input line will show you the function with left parentheses, @SUM(. Use the arrow keys to move to the first cell you wish to include, in this case D3. The cell address on the input line will change as you move through the cells, as it did for formulas.

4. To let Quattro Pro know what the starting point is, you must **anchor** the function. To do this, type a period when the starting cell—in this case, D3—is highlighted. The period is called the **pointer**. The input line now says "@SUM(D3..D3".

5. Use the ↓ key to move through the column. All the cells, starting with the starting cell, will be highlighted. The ending cell in the input line will change as you move down the column. A set of cells highlighted this way is called a **block**.

> **CAUTION:** If you try using the ↓ key without first anchoring the function with a period, the column won't be "fixed" at one end.

6. When you reach the ending cell, in this case D18, type **)** to complete the function.

The input line should read @SUM(D3..D18). (Refer to Figure 2-3.)

20 First Look at Quattro Pro 2.0/3.0

Figure 2-3
@ SUM function

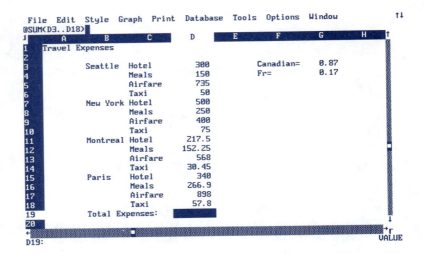

 CAUTION: Don't forget to type the right parenthesis at the end of a function. If you do forget, Quattro Pro gives you an error message prompting you for it. If you see the error message, first press Esc *to remove the message and then add the).*

Press Enter to have Quattro Pro calculate the answer, 4990.9. Note that the function correctly sums up the values even though some of the cells contain formulas referring to other cells rather than simple numbers.

CHANGING THE WAY VALUES ARE DISPLAYED

You now know that your total travel expenses were 4990.9. Wouldn't you prefer, though, to have the figure in currency format? In fact, wouldn't the entire column of figures be easier to read if it were in dollars and cents?

What you want to do, in other words, is change the **numeric format** of the numbers. Changing the numeric format is one of the menu choices, under the menu heading **Style**. You can modify the way numbers appear in a variety of ways, one of which is changing the number of decimal places that Quattro Pro displays. The numbers that you entered stay the same; only the way they are displayed on the screen or printed out is changed.

For this command, as for many others in Quattro Pro, you will be asked to specify a **block** of cells to be modified. One of the most important features of spreadsheet programs is that they allow you to work with groups of cells

Lesson 2/ Creating a Spreadsheet Application **21**

(called blocks) at once rather than requiring you to work with one cell at a time. Blocks can be any size, from a single cell (a "group" of one) to all the cells in a large spreadsheet. The one requirement is that the cells must form a rectangle; that is, they cannot be scattered all over the spreadsheet, nor can the cells in the block form an L or T shape. When you used the @SUM function, you specified a block consisting of cells in a single column. In later commands, you will specify blocks consisting of cells spread out over several columns and rows.

This time, you will convert the values in column D to currency format. Since changing formats is very common in spreadsheets, Quattro Pro provides you with shortcut keys so that you don't have to use the menu. Of course, if you forget the shortcuts, you can always pull down the menu! The shortcut for format is [Ctrl]-[F] (while holding down the [Ctrl] key, press [F]). Move to D19 if you are not there already, and

1. Press [Ctrl]-[F]

   (You could also have chosen /**Style** |Numeric Format from the menu).

   You will see a pop-up menu, which gives you a number of format choices.

2. Press **C** (for **C**urrency)

   (or press [↓] until Currency is highlighted, and press [Enter]).

   You will be prompted for the number of decimal places. Quattro Pro assumes you want 2; since that is the usual number for currency, just press [Enter].

   On the input line, you will see: "Block to be modified: D19..D19".

3. Press [↑] 16 times to extend the block up through D3. (You could also have anchored the block at D3 and moved down, as you did before.) The input line should now read "Block to be modified: D19..D3".

4. Press [Enter]

   Cells D3 through D19 should be in currency format.

But what has happened to Total Expenses in D19? All we can see is a row of asterisks (Figure 2-4)!

Don't worry. Nothing has happened to D19; if you check the input line, you'll see that the function is still entered correctly. The only problem is that adding the dollar sign, comma, and decimal places has made the value too wide for the column.

All you have to do to fix this problem is widen the column.

> **CAUTION: Whenever a formatted value is too wide for the existing column, Quattro Pro displays a row of asterisks in the cell.**

22   First Look at Quattro Pro 2.0/3.0

Figure 2-4
Column width too narrow for value

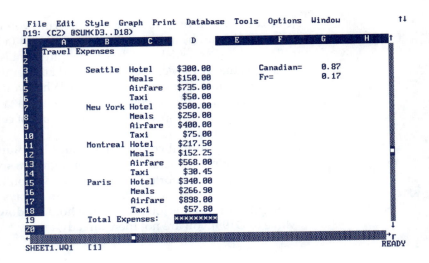

CHANGING COLUMN WIDTH

The menu choice that lets you change the width of columns, **Column Width**, is also under the **St**yle heading in the menu. It too has a shortcut key, Ctrl-W (while holding down the Ctrl key, press W). To change the width of a column:

1. Position yourself anywhere in that column, in this case D.

2. Press Ctrl-W

   (The menu choice is /**St**yle | **C**olumn Width.)

   The input line will say "Alter the width of the current column [1..254]: 9".

   This tells you that 9 is the current column width and that you can change it to any number between 1 and 254. Since 9 is too narrow, try 10.

3. Type **10** and press Enter

   You should see the entire spreadsheet adjust itself, and cell D19 will read $4,990.90.

Try converting the values in cells G3 and G4 to currency format on your own. When you are done, the spreadsheet should look like Figure 2-5 on the following page.

Congratulations! You have completed your first full spreadsheet application. We'll continue to work on this in the next lesson.

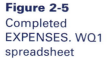

Figure 2-5
Completed
EXPENSES. WQ1
spreadsheet

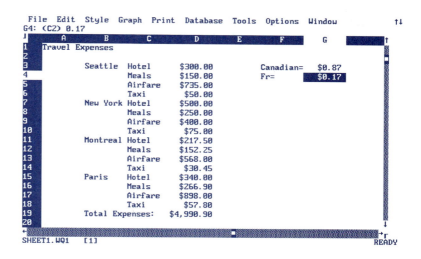

SHORTCUT KEY FOR SAVING FILES

You already know how to save a spreadsheet by choosing the **S**ave option from the **F**ile menu. The shortcut key for this is Ctrl-S (while holding down the Ctrl key, press S). To save your new spreadsheet with the name EXPENSES.WQ1,

1. Press Ctrl-S

2. Type **Expenses**

The file will be saved as EXPENSES.WQ1.

NOTE: If you wish to save the spreadsheet on a floppy disk, follow the instructions in Lesson One.

SHORTCUT KEY FOR EXITING QUATTRO PRO

The shortcut key for exiting Quattro Pro is Ctrl-X (while holding down the Ctrl key, press X). Press Ctrl-X and exit Quattro Pro.

24 First Look at Quattro Pro 2.0/3.0

■ *SUMMARY OF COMMANDS*

Topic or Feature	Command or Reference	Menu	Page
Absolute Cell Addresses	F4		16
Adding Cells	@SUM		18
Block	(Beginning cell address .. Ending cell address)		21
Column Width	Ctrl-W	/Style ¦ Column Width	22
Currency Format	Ctrl-F, C	/Style ¦ Numeric Format ¦ Currency	21
Enter Formulas Without Typing	Arrow keys		15
Exit Quattro Pro	Ctrl-X	/File ¦Exit	23
Function Menu	Alt-F3		18
Numeric Format	Ctrl-F	/Style ¦ Numeric Format	21
Pointer	..		18
Save Spreadsheet	Ctrl-S	/File ¦Save	23

■ *SELF-TEST*

1. You are at A1, with values 5 in B1 and 6 in C3. What steps would you follow to enter a formula that added the contents of B1 and C3? _____ _____.

2. In a formula, a(n) _____ cell address locates a cell by its position with respect to the formula.

3. In a formula, a(n) _____ cell address locates a cell at a specific cell address, regardless of its position with respect to the formula.

4. Press _____ to insert $s into the cell address in question 3.

Lesson 2/ Creating a Spreadsheet Application **25**

5. Describe the parts of the function @SUM(B1..B6), and explain what the function will do. _____

   _____ .

6. Press _____ to display a list of all Quattro Pro functions.

7. Press _____ to remove the list of Quattro Pro functions from the screen.

8. What steps would you follow to display cell contents in Currency format?

   _____ .

9. What does a row of asterisks in a cell mean? _____

   _____ .

10. What steps would you follow to correct the condition that produced the row of asterisks? _____

   _____ .

LESSON THREE: Editing a Spreadsheet

OBJECTIVES

At the end of this lesson you, will be able to:

- Display an already-existing spreadsheet.
- Change values and recalculate formulas.
- Insert and delete rows and columns.
- Copy the contents of a cell.
- Move the contents of a cell.
- Save a file after modifying it.

In the last lesson, you learned how to create a simple spreadsheet and how to use labels, values, formulas, and functions to get useful results. In this lesson, you will learn how to modify a spreadsheet to present information more clearly and get more useful results.

OPENING A SPREADSHEET

The first step is to display your spreadsheet, EXPENSES.WQ1. The command for this is the **O**pen command on the **/F**ile menu.

1. Select **/F**ile **|O**pen.

   You will see a box with the prompt: "Enter name of file to open:" and a list of available files (Figure 3-1).

2. Use the arrow keys to move the highlight to EXPENSES.WQ1.

3. Press [Enter].

> **CAUTION: These instructions assume you have saved the file on your hard disk. If you saved it on a floppy disk, you will not see it listed in the box. To retrieve it from a diskette in the A drive, first place the diskette in the drive. Then**
> **1. Press [Esc] [Esc] (to clear away the prompt for the default directory).**
> **2. Type A:EXPENSES.WQ1 and press [Enter]**

26

Figure 3-1
Opening a spreadsheet

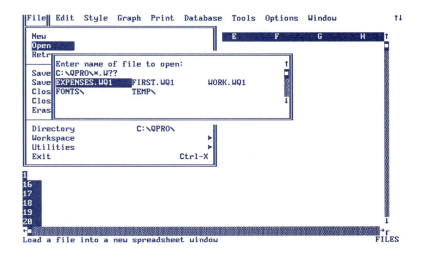

CHANGING VALUES IN A SPREADSHEET

It is extremely easy to change values in a spreadsheet. In fact, spreadsheets are designed to recalculate formulas quickly with new values. To see how, assume that, on reviewing your expenses, you find you made a mistake in typing them into the spreadsheet. Instead of spending $300 on your hotel in Seattle, you spent $316, and instead of spending $75 for taxis in New York, you spent $78.95.

To make these changes, all you have to do is move to the proper cells and edit the values.

1. Move to D3 (use F5, the Go To key).

2. Press F2 to enter Edit mode.

3. Change the value to **316**, and press Enter.

The spreadsheet will instantly recalculate your total expenses as $5,006.90. Note that the new value, 316, is automatically displayed in currency format.

Now change the New York taxi expenses to $78.95. Again, the spreadsheet will automatically recalculate the total, this time to $5,010.85.

You can see an even more dramatic example of the power of spreadsheets if you try to change values used in formulas. Suppose you discover that the exchange rate you used in calculating the value of Canadian dollars is wrong. A Canadian dollar is not worth $0.87 U.S.; instead, it is worth $0.89.

1. Move to G3.

2. Press F2 and edit the value to read 0.89.

28   First Look at Quattro Pro 2.0/3.0

Again, all the values will quickly be recalculated, with the total expenses now reading $5,020.05 (Figure 3-2).

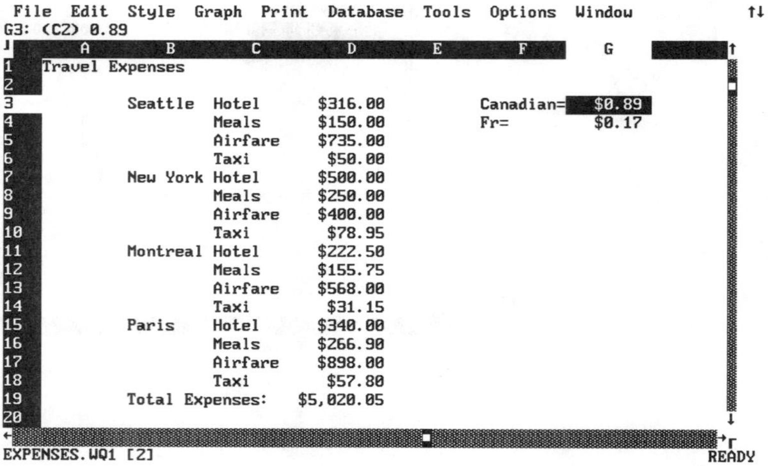

Figure 3-2
Changing a value
used in formulas

```
    File  Edit  Style  Graph  Print  Database  Tools  Options  Window          ↑↓
 G3: (C2) 0.89
    A        B        C          D         E        F          G              ↑
 1  Travel Expenses
 2
 3              Seattle   Hotel     $316.00          Canadian=   $0.89
 4                        Meals     $150.00          Fr=         $0.17
 5                        Airfare   $735.00
 6                        Taxi       $50.00
 7              New York  Hotel     $500.00
 8                        Meals     $250.00
 9                        Airfare   $400.00
10                        Taxi       $78.95
11              Montreal  Hotel     $222.50
12                        Meals     $155.75
13                        Airfare   $568.00
14                        Taxi       $31.15
15              Paris     Hotel     $340.00
16                        Meals     $266.90
17                        Airfare   $898.00
18                        Taxi       $57.80
19              Total Expenses:   $5,020.05
20
 EXPENSES.WQ1 [2]                                                        READY
```

· · · · · · · · · ·
INSERTING AND DELETING ROWS AND COLUMNS

There are other changes you may want to make in the spreadsheet. Suppose, for example, that you would like subtotals for each of the four trips. You already know how to use the @SUM formula to get the amounts. But where should you put the subtotals? Wouldn't it be nice to be able to put them on the line underneath the expenses for each city? To do this, you need to add some blank rows underneath each city's expenses. Quattro Pro allows you to insert rows in a spreadsheet, effectively pushing existing information down to make room for new information.

Inserting Rows

The command for inserting rows or columns is /Edit│Insert. The shortcut key is Ctrl-I (while holding down Ctrl, press I). To use this shortcut,

1. First, move to any cell in the row where you want to insert a blank line. It does not matter if there is information in that row; when you insert a new row, the existing information will be moved down. Move to A7.

2. Next, use the Insert command. Press Ctrl-I

   You will see a pop-up menu:

Lesson 3/ Editing a Spreadsheet **29**

Insert

Rows

Columns

Rows will be highlighted. This menu is asking whether you wish to insert rows or columns.

3. Since you want to insert rows, select **Rows**. Type **R**

The input line will read "Enter row insert block: A7..A7". This means that the starting block has already been anchored at A7. To insert rows, you use the arrow keys to move the highlight down to include the number of rows you wish to insert.

4. In this case, you want to insert two rows, one for the subtotal itself and one to separate Seattle Expenses from New York Expenses. In other words, you want to push the rest of the spreadsheet, starting with New York, down two rows. Press ⬇ once, so that two cells are highlighted. The input line will read: "Enter row insert block: A7..A8". Only the cells in column A will be highlighted, rather than all of rows 7 and 8.

5. Once the correct number of rows is highlighted (two in this case), press ⟨Enter⟩. The entire spreadsheet below your starting point will move down by the number of rows you inserted. Note that the highlight remains on the cell with which you started, A7. Now, though, rows 7 and 8 are blank. The label "New York", which was at cell B7, is now at cell B9, and the rest of the information has likewise moved down without any labels, values, or formulas changing.

Insert two rows after the New York, Montreal, and Paris expenses. When you are done, the top part of the spreadsheet will look like Figure 3-3.

Inserting Columns

You follow the same procedure to insert columns as you used to insert rows. First, place the highlight on any cell in the column where you want to add a blank. All the information in that column will be moved to the right. Try this in column E.

1. Place the highlight at cell E7 (you can place it in any cell in column E).

2. Press ⟨Ctrl⟩-⟨I⟩

3. This time, when you see the pop-up menu, type **C** to choose to insert a column.

When you see: "Enter column insert block: E7..E7" on the input line, use ➡ to move the highlight to include the number of columns you wish to insert.

30   First Look at Quattro Pro 2.0/3.0

Figure 3-3
Inserting lines

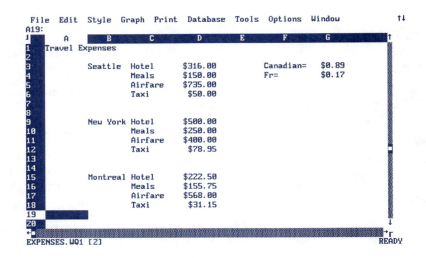

4. Insert two columns this time: Press →

   The input line will read: "Enter column insert block: E7..F7".

5. Press Enter

   Look at the screen. No, the information on Canadian and French currency has not disappeared! Quattro Pro moved it to the right, to columns H and I, to make room for the two blank columns you just inserted.

6. Press Ctrl-→ to see the information on Canadian and French currency.

7. Press Ctrl-← to return to the rest of the spreadsheet.

Deleting Columns   Since you don't need those extra columns now, get rid of them by deleting them. The command for deleting rows and columns is /Edit !Delete. The steps for deleting rows and columns are very similar to those for inserting them, but there is no shortcut key—and for a very good reason.

> **CAUTION:** *If you delete a row or a column, you delete everything in it. Delete only rows or columns that you are sure you want to get rid of. Quattro Pro, unlike some word processors, will not prompt you to make sure you really meant to delete a section of your work.*

To delete the two columns you just inserted:

1. Move to E7.

Lesson 3/ Editing a Spreadsheet   **31**

2. Press /**Edit** ¦**Delete**

   You will again see the pop-up menu, this time asking if you wish to delete **R**ows or **C**olumns.

3. Press **C** to choose **C**olumns. The input line will read: "Delete one or more columns: E7..E7".

4. Press ⟶ to highlight two columns.

   The input line will read: "Delete one or more columns: E7..F7".

5. Since that is what you wish to do, accept the choice. Press ⟨Enter⟩

   The spreadsheet will go back to its earlier form.

. . . .
SUBTOTALS: MORE ABOUT FORMULAS

Having used Insert to make room for the calculation of subtotals, you can now enter the subtotals into the spreadsheet. You already know how to place each subtotal directly underneath the cells with each city's expenses. The spreadsheet would be easier to read, though, if the subtotals were set off slightly, so why not put them one cell to the right? This involves placing the @SUM function one column to the right of the cells to be added, but as you will see, the procedure is the same:

1. Move to B7. Type **Seattle Expenses:** and press ⟨Enter⟩

2. Move to E7, where you want to place the formula.

3. Press ⟨Alt⟩-⟨F3⟩ to bring up the function menu.

   (a) Select @SUM by highlighting it and pressing ⟨Enter⟩

   (b) Move to D3.

4. Type a period to indicate the start of the block to be added.

5. Move down the column to D6, the last cell in the block.

   Type **)** to end the function.

6. Press ⟨Enter⟩ to calculate the subtotal and return to E7.

7. Use ⟨Ctrl⟩-⟨F⟩, discussed in Lesson Two, to change the numeric format of the cell to currency.

   (a) Press ⟨Ctrl⟩-⟨F⟩

   (b) Select **C**urrency

32 First Look at Quattro Pro 2.0/3.0

(c) Specify two decimal places, and press [Enter]

Since the value is now too large, you will see a row of asterisks in E7. Use [Ctrl]-[W] to change the column width. This time, instead of guessing the width that would eliminate the asterisks, you can let Quattro Pro help you by pressing [→] until the asterisks disappear.

8. To try this,

(a) Press [Ctrl]-[W]

(b) The input line prompts you for the new column width. Press [→]

(c) The asterisks disappear, and the input line specifies that the new column width is 10 characters. Since column E is now wide enough to display the value you want, press [Enter]

Cell E7 should now show the correct value, $1,251.00.

COPYING CELLS

You could now repeat the entire procedure just outlined for each city. Once again, though, Quattro Pro can save you time and energy by allowing you to copy cells. The command for this is /Edit¦Copy; the shortcut key is [Ctrl]-[C].

Copying and Modifying Labels

Since the label you want to use for the New York subtotal, "New York Expenses:", is very similar to the label you already have, "Seattle Expenses:", you can save effort by copying and editing the label. To copy,

1. Move to the cell you want to copy, B7. Press [Ctrl]-[C]. (You could also have selected /Edit¦Copy). The input line will read: "Source block of cells: B7..B7".

2. Since you want to copy only cell B7 this time, press [Enter]

   The input line will read: "Destination for cells: B7".

3. Move to the cell you wish to copy the information to, in this case B13. You have to use the cursor movement keys to move the highlight; [F5] won't work here.

   The input line will read: "Destination for cells: B13".

4. Press [Enter]

B13 will now read "Seattle Expenses:" and the highlight will be back where you started at B7.

5. Edit the new label at B13:

   (a) Move to B13.

   (b) Press [F2], and edit the contents of the cell to read "New York Expenses:"

6. Follow the same procedure to copy and modify labels for subtotals for Montreal and Paris. The label for Montreal expenses should go in B19; the label for Paris expenses should go in B25. Refer to Figure 3-4.

Figure 3-4
Using @SUM for subtotals

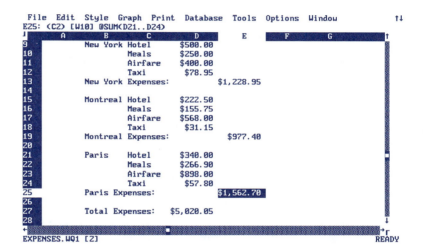

Copying Numbers

Use precisely the same procedure to copy numbers as you used to copy labels. When you copy a cell with numbers, you also copy all the formats that go along with that cell.

Copying Formulas and Functions with Cell Addresses

Copying formulas and functions with cell addresses is a little more complicated. If a formula contains an absolute cell address, it will continue to refer to that cell address even if it is copied to another part of the spreadsheet. But if a formula contains a relative cell address, the formula will always refer to

34   First Look at Quattro Pro 2.0/3.0

whatever cell is in the same relative position. For example, if a formula referring to a cell three columns to the right and eight rows up is copied to a new position, it will continue to refer to whatever cell is three columns to the right and eight rows up from its new position. In some cases, that is exactly what you want it to do; in other cases, though, you may have to modify the formula.

Look at the formula in cell E7 by moving to E7 and looking at the input line. The formula uses relative cell addresses. If you wish to copy it to get subtotals for the other cities, you must copy it to a cell with the same position relative to the cells you wish to add.

It is easy to demonstrate why. Using the same procedure you used to copy labels, copy the formula in cell E7 to E13.

1. Move to E7.

2. Press Ctrl - C

3. Press Enter to designate E7 as the source block of cells.

4. Move to E13, the destination block.

5. Press Enter

The spreadsheet will calculate New York expenses as $1,228.95

Move to E13, and look at the formula on the input line. You will see that the formula has been automatically changed to point to cells D9..D12. You can also see that all formatting has been copied with the formula.

What happens if you make a mistake and do not position the new formula correctly? Try this by copying the formula in E13 to D13, using the procedure you just learned. The result in D13 will be $0.00, and if you move to D13 and look at the formula on the input line, you will see why. The cell addresses in the formula have been automatically changed to retain the same relative position to the formula itself and now refer to cells C9..C12. Since those cells don't contain any values, their sum is 0.

Press Del to delete the formula since you have no need for an incorrect formula in the spreadsheet.

Copy the formula in E13 to E19 and E25 to get subtotals for Montreal and Paris expenses. When you are done, the bottom part of the spreadsheet should look like Figure 3-4.

. . . .
MOVING THE CONTENTS OF A CELL

You have now found subtotals for the expenses in each city. In the process, the spreadsheet has become a little unbalanced, since the value for Total Expenses

Lesson 3/ Editing a Spreadsheet **35**

is still located in the column with individual expenses (column D), not under the subtotals in column E.

That can easily be changed by using the Move command on the Edit menu: /**Edit** ¦**M**ove. The shortcut key is Ctrl-M. The command is very similar to the Copy command. To move the formula for Total Expenses, now in D27, to E27,

1. Move to D27. Press Ctrl-M

   The prompt on the input line should look familiar since it will read: "Source block of cells: D27..D27".

2. Press Enter to accept D27.

   The input line will read: "Destination for cells: D27".

3. Move to E27.

   The input line will read: "Destination for cells: E27".

4. Press Enter. Cell E27 will display the value for Total Expenses, $5,020.05, and cell D27 will be empty.

If you move to cell E27 and look at the input line, you can see that this time Quattro Pro did not adjust the cell addresses. Since you used the Move rather than the Copy command, Quattro Pro assumed you wanted the formula to refer to the same cell addresses.

You have now learned basic spreadsheet editing skills. Save EXPENSES.WQ1; you'll use it to explore more advanced editing skills in the next lesson.

. . . .
SAVING A FILE AFTER MODIFYING IT

Since you saved this file at the end of the last chapter, Quattro Pro compares the new version with the old one before saving it. If there are changes, as there are in this case, Quattro Pro presents you with a slightly different pop-up menu when you try to save the file, asking whether you want to keep the old version or replace it with the new one.

1. Press Ctrl-S to save the file.

   You will see the new pop-up menu (shown in Figure 3-5).

2. Type **R** to **R**eplace the existing file with the new changes you have made. (You could also press ↓ until **R**eplace is highlighted and press Enter.) This will save the new version of EXPENSES.WQ1.

Now you are ready to leave Quattro Pro by pressing Ctrl-X.

Figure 3-5
Saving a spreadsheet after modifying it

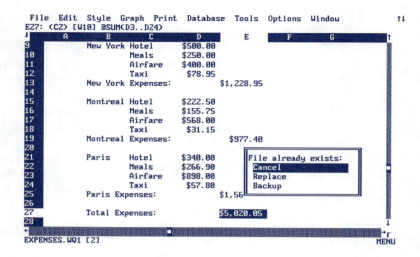

■ SUMMARY OF COMMANDS

Topic or Feature	Command or Reference	Menu	Page
Copy a Cell	Ctrl-C	/Edit |Copy	32
Delete a Column	Delete	/Edit |Delete | Column	31
Delete a Row	Delete	/Edit |Delete | Row	30
Insert a Column	Ctrl-I, C	/Edit |Insert | Column	29
Insert a Row	Ctrl-I, R	/Edit |Insert | Row	28
Move a Cell	Ctrl-M	/Edit |Move	35
Open an Existing Spreadsheet	Open	/File |Open	26
Save a Spreadsheet after Changing It	Ctrl-S, R	/File |Save | Replace	35

■ SELF-TEST

1. List three commands you have used that are found on the /**File** menu.

Lesson 3/ Editing a Spreadsheet **37**

2. List four commands you have used that are found on the /Edit menu.

   _____ .

3. When Quattro Pro inserts more than one row, do the new rows appear

   above or below the row containing the highlight? _____

   _____ .

4. When Quattro Pro inserts more than one column, do the new columns
   appear to the left or to the right of the column containing the highlight?

   _____ .

5. Cell C1 contains the formula +B4*K16. If you use Ctrl-C to copy it to C5,

   will the new formula in C5 be different? If so, what will it be? _____

   _____ .

6. Cell C1 contains the formula +B4*K16. If you use Ctrl-C to copy it to

   C5, will the new formula in C5 be different? If so, what will it be?_____

   _____

   _____ .

7. Cell C1 contains the formula +D17-D16. If you use Ctrl-M to move it to

   C5, will the new formula in C5 be different? If so, what will it be? _____

   _____ .

8. If you wish to save an already-existing spreadsheet after modifying it,
   which of the following options should you choose?

   Replace

   Cancel

   Backup

   _____ .

9. What steps should you follow if you want to exit Quattro Pro without

   saving modifications to the spreadsheet? _____

   _____ .

LESSON FOUR
Advanced Editing Techniques

OBJECTIVES

At the end of this lesson, you will be able to:

- Copy a block of cells.
- Use Extended Mode to define a block.
- Move a block of cells.
- Draw single lines, double lines, and boxes.
- Print a block of cells.
- Delete a block of cells.

In the last lesson, you modified the EXPENSES.WQ1 spreadsheet to get subtotals by city. Imagine now that you want to itemize business travel expenses as deductions on your tax forms. To do that, you have to separate the expenses into Meals and All Other Expenses since the Internal Revenue Service will allow you to deduct only 80% of your expenses for meals and entertainment.

You could rearrange your current spreadsheet, but then you would lose the correct subtotals. Fortunately, you have another choice: Since a spreadsheet can contain so many cells, you can copy the information to another part of the spreadsheet and work with it there. To do this,

1. Open the spreadsheet.

2. Select /**File** |**O**pen and choose EXPENSES.WQ1.

3. Choose a new section of the spreadsheet. The rest of this lesson assumes you have chosen the section immediately below the section with travel expenses.

4. Move to A30, type **Travel Expenses, for Tax Purposes**, and press ⏎Enter

5. Move to A32, type **Meals and Entertainment:** and press ⏎Enter

6. Move to D32, type **All Other Expenses:** and press ⏎Enter

Now you have to make a decision. You could copy the information, bit by bit, to the proper category in the new section of the spreadsheet. For example, you could first copy all the Meals expenses to column A, starting at row 31, and then go back and copy all Hotel, Airfare, and Taxi expenses to column D at row 33. That would give you the desired result. Or, you could copy all the

38

information currently in columns C and D to the All Other Expenses column, column D, and then rearrange it as necessary. That too would give you the desired result and save some jumping around the spreadsheet. It would also protect your completed work from accidental copying and deleting mistakes.

For this example, choose the second alternative, and copy all the information you will need to the new section. You already know how to copy one cell; copying many cells is very similar. You do not need to copy city names for this project, but you will need to copy labels indicating the types of expenses.

1. Move to C3, the first cell containing expenses.

2. Press [Ctrl]–[C] to select the copy command.

    The input line will read: "Source block of cells: C3..C3".

3. If you only wanted to copy a single cell, C3, you would just press [Enter]. Since you want to copy many cells, though, you need to specify a *block* of cells to copy. Do this as follows:

    (a) Position the highlight on the first cell in the block (C3, in this case).

    (b) Use the arrow keys to extend the block to cover all the cells you wish to copy.

4. From C3, use the arrow keys to extend the block to cover all the expenses and labels, ending with D24.

    The input line will read (refer to Figure 4-1): "Source block of cells: C3..D24".

Figure 4-1
Block of cells to copy

Since that is the block you wish to copy, press [Enter]

40 First Look at Quattro Pro 2.0/3.0

5. The input line will now prompt you for the destination for the block, which is the cell where you wish to place the upper left corner of the block (the starting cell). The most convenient place to put the block is D33, so position the highlight there.

6. Move to D33.

   The input line will read: "Destination for cells: D33".

7. Press ⌞Enter⌟

   The expenses will be copied.

8. After copying, Quattro Pro will automatically position you back at the starting cell of the block you copied, in case you want to copy something else. Since you do not, move to D33, and look at your new copy. You may wish to move over to A30 to get a better perspective.

9. To make this information presentable, you must do the following:

   (a) Move all the Meals expenses to columns A and B.

   (b) Eliminate the blank lines from the All Other Expenses column.

   (c) Sum up both columns.

You can do all this with the copying, moving, and deleting techniques you know. One editing shortcut, though, makes it much easier: using ⌞Shift⌟-⌞F7⌟ to enter **Extended mode**. Extended mode lets you specify a block of cells first and then move, copy, or delete it. With this technique you can cut and paste in a spreadsheet, very much as you do in a word processor. You can use ⌞Shift⌟-⌞F7⌟ with any command that requires you to specify a block.

EXTENDED MODE

To specify a block using Extended mode,

1. Move to the first cell in the block.

2. Press ⌞Shift⌟-⌞F7⌟ (while holding down the ⌞Shift⌟ key, press ⌞F7⌟).

   You will see EXT appear on the bottom right of the screen.

3. Use the arrow keys to extend the block to all the cells you wish to include.

Try this now.

1. Move to the first Meals label at D34.

Lesson 4 / Advanced Editing Techniques   41

You would like to move it, and the amount in cell E34, to A33 (just underneath Meals and Entertainment).

(a) Press [Shift]-[F7]

(b) Press [→]

Both Meals and $150.00 should be highlighted.

2. To move this block, press [Ctrl]-[M] (or select /Edit ¦ **Move**). Note that you are not prompted for the source block because you have already specified it using Extended mode. Instead, you are prompted for the Destination for cells.

3. Since you wish to move the cells to A33, use the arrow keys to position the highlight there.

   (a) Move to A33.

   (b) Press [Enter]

The Meals expenses will have moved from D34 and E34 to A33 and B33.

> **CAUTION:** What if you make a mistake and block the wrong set of cells? If you realize your error before you try to copy or move the cells, just press [Esc].

That leaves you with a blank line between Hotel and Airfare expenses. Delete it, using the technique you learned in the last lesson. Assuming you are at D34,

1. Select /Edit ¦ **Delete**.

2. Select **R**ows.

3. Press [Enter] to confirm the deletion of row 34.

   This moves up the rest of the information in columns D and E.

4. Using [Shift]-[F7] and the Move and Delete commands, move all the Meals expenses to columns A and B, and delete the blank lines from columns D and E. When you are done, this section of the spreadsheet will look like Figure 4-2.

Now, all you have to do is add up the columns, something you are very good at by now.

1. Type **Total:** in cells A37 and D45.

2. Using the @SUM function, place the total expenses for each column in cells B37 and E45.

Figure 4-2
Expenses after moving cells and deleting lines

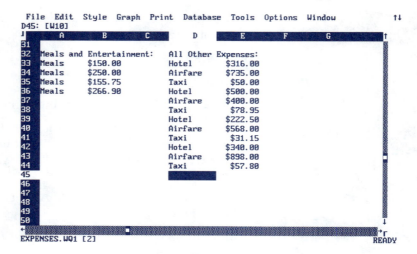

3. Use the /**Style** !**Numeric Format** command, Ctrl-F, to change the value to currency format, with two decimal places.

To make sure you are completely prepared for tax time, you can even calculate your allowable deduction for meals and entertainment.

1. Move to A39.

2. Type **Allowable Deduction:**

3. Move to B40. Insert the formula you need to calculate 80% of the total meals and entertainment expenses, +B37*.8.

You learned how to enter formulas in Lesson One. If you need a reminder, though, here it is:

1. Type +

2. Move the highlight to cell B37.

3. Type *.8

4. Press Enter

5. Press Ctrl-F to change cell B40 to currency format, with two decimal places.

The completed section will look like Figure 4-3.

LINES AND BOXES

Another kind of advanced editing technique does not help with calculation, but it does make spreadsheets easier to read. The technique involves drawing

Figure 4-3
Eighty percent of meals and entertainment expenses

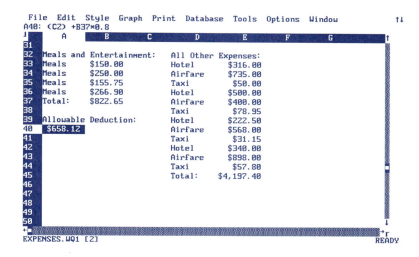

lines and boxes to clarify or enhance data presentation. To see how this approach works, return to the first page of the spreadsheet (the easiest way to do this is to press [Home] to return to A1).

The command for Line Drawing is on the /**S**tyle menu. The basic procedure is simple.

1. Use [Shift]-[F7] to specify the cells where you want to draw the line or box. (If you do not specify the block first, Quattro Pro will prompt you for the block when you select the Line Drawing command.)

2. Select /**S**tyle ¦ Line Drawing. An additional two menus appear. Menu 1 lets you choose the position of the line or box (refer to Figure 4-4). Menu 2 lets you choose the type of line to draw. Line types are:

Figure 4-4
Position menu for line drawing

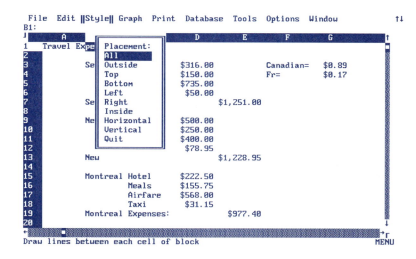

44   First Look at Quattro Pro 2.0/3.0

None

Single

Double

Thick

The line type you have specified will appear in the block.

Remember when drawing lines and boxes that a little spreadsheet enhancement goes a long way. Too many lines and boxes will make it harder, not easier, to understand your data.

For this example, you will draw only simple lines and one box. You will place double underlines under the title, single lines between subgroups, and a double-lined box around the total amount of expenses.

To place a double underline under the title,

1. Move to A1 if you are not there already.

2. Use Shift-F7 to block Travel Expenses.

3. Select /**S**tyle ¦**L**ine Drawing.

4. Type **B** (for **B**ottom).

5. Type **D** (for **D**ouble).

6. Type **Q** (to **Q**uit the /**S**tyle menu).

Travel Expenses now has a double underline. To place a single underline under the row with Seattle Expenses (row 7),

1. Move to B7.

2. Use Shift-F7 to block the row through E7.

3. Select /**S**tyle ¦**L**ine Drawing.

4. Select **B**ottom.

5. Select **S**ingle.

6. Select **Q**uit.

Follow the same procedure to insert lines underneath the rows with New York Expenses (B13 through E13), Montreal Expenses (B19 through E19), and Paris Expenses (B25 through E25).

To place a double-lined box around the cell with total expenses, E27,

1. Move to E27.

2. Press Shift-F7

3. Select /**S**tyle ¦**L**ine Drawing.

4. Select **O**utside.

5. Select **D**ouble.

Lesson 4/ Advanced Editing Techniques   45

6. Select **Q**uit.

Oh no! There is another row of asterisks in cell E27!

You know what to do about them. Use [Ctrl]-[W] to increase the width of the column to 11, and you will see the total amount again, enclosed in a double-lined box. When you are done, this section of the spreadsheet will look like Figure 4-5.

Figure 4-5
Lines and boxes

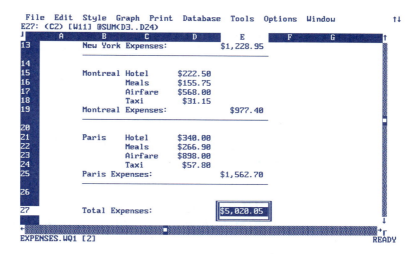

> **CAUTION:** You cannot delete lines and boxes by pressing [Del], as you can with ordinary spreadsheet data. If the line is in a row or column that is otherwise completely empty, you can use /Edit¦Delete to delete the row or column, which will remove the line. (This will remove the line even if the row or column contains data, but it will also remove all the data!)

Deleting Lines and Boxes

To remove the line but not data (do not do this now),

1. Use [Shift]-[F7] to specify the block from which to remove the line.

2. Select the same /**S**tyle ¦Line Drawing ¦Line Position as you used to draw the line.

3. Select **N**one from the Line Type menu.

PRINTING A SECTION OF A SPREADSHEET

CAUTION: *This section should be tried only if Quattro Pro has been set up for a default printer, if the computer is connected to a printer, and if the printer is turned on.*

Often the only way to examine a spreadsheet properly is to print it out. You already know the basic techniques for printing out a section of the spreadsheet; in Lesson Ten you will learn more advanced printing techniques.

First, block the section of the spreadsheet you wish to print. Try this on the first part of the spreadsheet:

1. Press [Home] to move to A1.
2. Use [Shift]-[F7] to extend the block through F28.
3. Next, define the block to be printed. Select /**Print**|**Block**.

CAUTION: *If you try to print a spreadsheet without specifying a block first, you will see an error message, "No block defined." Press [Esc] to remove the message from the screen, and select /Print|Block to specify a block.*

4. Check to make sure that the **D**estination on the /**P**rint menu is set to **G**raphics Printer, or the lines you created will not print properly. If it is not,

   (a) Type **D** (for **D**estination).

   (b) Type **G** (for **G**raphics printer).

   Destination on the /**P**rint menu should now be set to Graphics Printer.

5. Print the block: Select **S**preadsheet print from the /**P**rint menu.

The section of the spreadsheet you specified should be printed.

To print the entire spreadsheet, first follow the directions in steps 1 and 2 to specify the block to be printed as A1 to G45. Then select **S**preadsheet print to print it.

DELETING A SECTION OF A SPREADSHEET

You can also use [Shift]-[F7] to define a block to delete. This is a quick way to delete a section of the spreadsheet (do not do this now).

Lesson 4/ Advanced Editing Techniques **47**

1. Move to the first cell of the block you want to delete.
2. Press [Shift]-[F7] to enter Extended mode.
3. Use the arrow keys to extend the block through the entire section you want to delete.
4. Press [Del]. The block will be deleted.

This concludes the lesson. Press [Ctrl]-[S] to save the spreadsheet, and specify **R**eplace. Then press [Ctrl]-[X] to exit.

■ *SUMMARY OF COMMANDS*

Topic or Feature	Command or Reference	Menu	Page
Copy a Block of Cells	Mark the block, [Ctrl]-[C]	/Edit ¦Copy	39
Delete a Block of Cells	Mark the block, [Del]		45
Draw Single-Lined Boxes	Line Drawing	/Style ¦Line Drawing ¦ Outside ¦ Single	44
Draw Double-Lined Boxes	Line Drawing	/Style ¦Line Drawing ¦ Outside ¦ Double	44
Draw Double Lines	Line Drawing	/Style ¦ Line Drawing Bottom ¦ Double	44
Draw Single Lines Below Cells	Line Drawing	/Style ¦Line Drawing ¦ Bottom ¦ Single	44
Mark a Block of Cells (Extended Mode)	[Shift]-[F7]		40
Move a Block of Cells	Mark the block, [Ctrl]-[M]	/Edit ¦Move	41
Set Up a Block to Print	Print	/Print ¦Block	46
Print a Block	Print	/Print ¦ Spreadsheet Print	46

48   First Look at Quattro Pro 2.0/3.0

■ *SELF-TEST*

1. List three commands you used that are found on the /Style menu. _____

   _____ .

2. A _____ is a group of cells forming a rectangle.

3. What is the advantage of using the answer to Question 2 in commands and formulas? _____

   _____ .

4. Press _____ to enter Extended Mode.

5. What steps would you follow to place a double line underneath E5..G5?

   _____

   _____ .

6. What steps would you follow to remove a double line from underneath E5..G5? _____

   _____ .

7. What steps could you follow to remove a double line from underneath E5..G5, assuming row 5 is blank? _____

   _____ .

8. To print a spreadsheet with a double-lined box, what must Destination on the /Print menu be set for? _____

   _____ .

9. To print cells A1..C15, what must **B**lock on the /Print menu be set for?

   _____

   _____ .

10. What should you do if you see "No block specified" on the screen while trying to print? _____

    _____ .

LESSON FIVE More About Functions

OBJECTIVES

At the end of this lesson, you will be able to:

- Change the alignment of cell contents.
- Display values in comma (financial) format.
- Display values in percent format.
- Use @COUNT, @MAX, and @MIN functions.
- Use the @PMT function to calculate monthly payments on a loan.
- Create links between different sections of a spreadsheet.
- Insert an absolute cell reference into a function.
- Use Solve For to work backward from the desired result of a formula to the conditions needed to produce that result.
- Recalculate a value produced by Solve For.
- Reset Solve For values.
- Use the @IF function to test for certain conditions.

In this lesson, you will use some of Quattro Pro's techniques for decision making. Since Quattro Pro can recalculate formulas so quickly, you can use its built-in functions, together with editing and copying techniques, to "plug in" a range of different values to the same formula. You can also use a special feature called Solve For, which lets you decide what result you would like to get from a formula and calculate backward to see what the variables should be. This lesson also introduces a few more techniques for enhancing the appearance of a spreadsheet.

For this lesson, imagine that you are in the market for a classic car. You expect to need a loan to pay for it and want to calculate the monthly payments to make sure you can afford them. The first step is to create a spreadsheet showing the list of cars you are interested in. Figure 5-1 shows the completed spreadsheet. Follow these steps to create the spreadsheet:

1. To enter the title, make sure [Caps Lock] is on.

    (a) Move to D1.

    (b) Type **CLASSIC CARS** and press [Enter]

2. To enter the column headings, move to A3.

    (a) In A3, type **MAKE** and press [Enter]

49

Figure 5-1
Classic.WQ1
spreadsheet

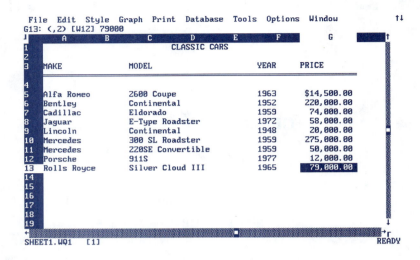

(b) In C3, type **MODEL** and press Enter

(c) In F3, type **YEAR** and press Enter

(d) In G3, type **PRICE** and press Enter

(e) Press Caps Lock again to turn it off.

3. Add a double line under the column headings:

(a) Move to A3, and press Shift-F7. Use → to extend the block to G3.

(b) Select /**S**tyle |**L**ine Drawing |**B**ottom |**D**ouble Line to insert a double line.

(c) Type **Q** (for **Q**uit) to leave the /**S**tyle menu.

4. Move to A5, and enter the following information in cells A5 through G13.

CAUTION: *Some of the model names begin with numbers, so you must first type an apostrophe (') to let Quattro Pro know you are typing a label, not a number. The ' will not appear in the cell, but it will appear on the input line when the cell is highlighted.*

	A	C	F	G
5	Alfa Romeo	'2600 Coupe	1963	14500
6	Bentley	Continental	1952	220000
7	Cadillac	Eldorado	1959	74000
8	Jaguar	E-Type Roadster	1972	58000

9	Lincoln	Continental	1948	20000
10	Mercedes	'300 SL Roadster	1959	275000
11	Mercedes	'220SE Convertible	1959	50000
12	Porsche	'911S	1977	12000
13	Rolls Royce	Silver Cloud III	1965	79000

Once the data are entered, you can change the appearance to make the result easier to read. The years, for example, are all right-aligned because Quattro Pro assumes you are entering values you might want to add in a column. Since you have no reason for adding years and the column would be easier to read if the years were left-aligned under the column title, you can now format them for left alignment.

CHANGING ALIGNMENT

The command for changing alignment is /Style |Alignment; the shortcut is Ctrl-A.

To change the alignment for the YEAR column,

1. Block the cells to be aligned.

2. Move to F5, and press Shift-F7; then extend the block through F13.

3. Press Ctrl-A.

   A pop-up menu appears with the following choices:

   General

   Left

   Right

   Center

4. Since you want left alignment, select Left.

   The years will be left-aligned.

COMBINING CURRENCY AND COMMA (FINANCIAL) FORMAT IN A COLUMN

The final task is to format the car prices. You already know how to use the /Style |Numeric Format command (Ctrl-F). Use it to format the first price in

52 First Look at Quattro Pro 2.0/3.0

the column (in G5) for currency; format the rest of the cells, G6 through G13, for comma (,) financial format. Since, as you know, formatting will require you to increase the width of the columns, start by changing the column width to 12.

1. Move to G5.

2. Press Ctrl-W

3. Type **12** and press Enter when prompted for the width.

4. Next, change the format of G5 to currency.

   (a) Press Ctrl-F

   (b) Select Currency .

   (c) Press Enter (to accept two decimal places).

   (d) Press Enter (to accept the specified block) .

5. Finally, change the block G6..G13 to comma format.

   (a) Move to G6, and press Shift-F7 . Extend the block through G13.

   (b) Press Ctrl-F

   (c) Type , (for comma format).

   (d) Press Enter (to accept two decimal places).

Column G is formatted, and the spreadsheet is complete. Refer to Figure 5-1.

USING @COUNT, @MAX, AND @MIN FUNCTIONS

In this example, you can easily count the total number of cars in the list and find the highest- and lowest-priced cars. If you had a very long list, though, or one that changed often, you would find it much harder to obtain those figures. For that reason, Quattro Pro provides functions to keep track of the information for you. @COUNT(cell block) counts the number of items in the specified block, @MAX(cell block) finds the highest value in the specified block, and @MIN(cell block) finds the lowest value in the specified block.

To see how these functions work,

1. Move to A15 and enter the following labels:

	A
15	**Number of Cars:**
16	**Highest Price:**
17	**Lowest Price:**

Lesson 5/ More About Functions **53**

2. Move to C15.

3. Press Alt-F3 to bring up the Function menu.

4. Select COUNT.

5. Move to the first car on the list, at A5.

6. Type a period.

7. Move to the last car on the list, at A13.

8. Type) to complete the formula.

9. Press Enter

@COUNT shows that there are nine cars in the specified block, which is correct.

To calculate the maximum price,

1. Move to C16.

2. Press Alt-F3 to bring up the Function menu.

3. Select MAX.

4. Move to the first price on the list, at G5.

5. Type a period.

6. Move to the last price on the list, at G13.

7. Type) to complete the formula.

8. Press Enter

9. Use Ctrl-F to format the cell for currency, with two decimal places.

The maximum price on the list is $275,000.00 (the Mercedes 300 SL). To calculate the minimum price,

1. Move to C17.

2. Press Alt-F3 to bring up the Function menu.

3. Select MIN.

4. Move to the first price on the list, at G5.

5. Type a period.

6. Move to the last price on the list, at G13.

7. Type) to complete the formula.

8. Press Enter

9. Press Ctrl-F to specify comma format, with two decimal places.

The minimum price on the list is $12,000.00 (the Porsche 911S). Refer to Figure 5-2.

Figure 5-2
@COUNT, @MAX, and @MIN functions

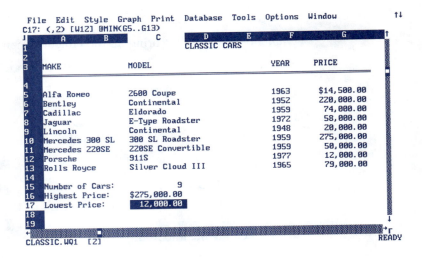

Now that you have calculated the number of cars, highest price, and lowest price, you can move on to finding monthly payments.

USING THE @PMT FUNCTION

To find the monthly payments for each car, you can use Quattro Pro's built-in @PMT function. @PMT calculates monthly payments given the amount of the loan (the principal), the monthly interest rate, and the number of payment periods (the term). The structure is @PMT(principal, interest rate, number of payment periods).

NOTE: @PMT can be adjusted to fit other time periods—for example, quarterly or annual payments—but in that case the interest rate and payment periods must also be quarterly or annual.

To illustrate this feature, assume that you are able to arrange financing for a potential classic car purchase at 8.5% annual interest over a 4-year period. To make calculation easier, enter the information in a separate area of the spreadsheet, cells A19 through C21. Note that C20 contains a formula.

	A	B	C
19	Interest, annual:		0.085
20	Interest, monthly:		+C19/12
21	Term (in months):		48

Use Ctrl-F (or /Style Numeric Format) to display the percentages in C19 and C20 in percentage format:

Lesson 5/ More About Functions **55**

1. Move to C19, press Shift-F7 , and extend the block to C20.
2. Press Ctrl -F to bring up the **Numeric** Format menu.
3. Select **Percent**.
4. Specify one decimal place.
5. Move to C23.

You will enter the formula into cell C23. Start with the price of the Alfa Romeo for the principal. The completed formula will be @PMT(G5,C20,C21). To enter the formula (move to C23 if you are not there already),

1. Press Alt -F3 to bring up the Function menu.
2. Select PMT.
3. Use the arrow keys to move to G5.
4. Type ,
5. Use the arrow keys to move to C20.
6. Type ,
7. Use the arrow keys to move to C21.
8. Type) to complete the formula.
9. Press Enter to calculate the value, 357.4004.

To have it displayed in currency format, use Ctrl -F , and specify currency, two decimal places. The value is now displayed as $357.40.

CREATING LINKS BETWEEN DIFFERENT PARTS OF THE SPREADSHEET

The last step is to add a label that clarifies what car the monthly payment is for. As usual, you have choices. You could type the name of the car, or you could copy the label in A5 to E23. In each case, the new label would have no further connection, or **link**, to the original list. A third possibility, which would preserve the link, is to enter the cell address of the original label (+A5). That would preserve its connection to the original list and be especially useful in copying, as we will see later in the lesson. To add the label,

1. Move to cell E23.
2. Type **+A5** and press Enter

Alfa Romeo will appear in cell E23.

56 First Look at Quattro Pro 2.0/3.0

To copy the model,

1. Move to G23 .

2. Type **+C5** and press `Enter`

2600 Coupe will appear in cell G23.

COPYING FUNCTIONS

To calculate the monthly payments for the other cars, you could redo or edit the formula, substituting the cell address for the new car price you wish to calculate. That is, instead of G5 in the formula @PMT(G5,C20,C21), you could edit the function to use G6 if you wished to calculate monthly payments for the Bentley or G10 if you wished to calculate monthly payments for the Mercedes 300SL Roadster.

A more systematic way to proceed, though, is to copy the formula eight times, applying the formula to each remaining car on the list in turn. The procedure is similar to the one you used in the last lesson. The source block would be the cell containing the formula; the destination block would consist of as many cells as you want copied—in this case eight. As you know, however, copying functions and formulas requires special care to make sure that the formula continues to refer to the correct cell address after it is copied.

Move to C23, and look at the formula on the input line. If the formula were copied to C24—one row down—all the cell addresses would also move down one row. For example, G5 would become G6, C20 would become C21, and C21 would become C22. If the formula were copied two rows down, the cell addresses would become G7, C22, and C23. In the case of the cell address for the principal of the loan, the change would be useful because the changing cell addresses would move down the list of car prices. In the case of the interest rate and number of payment periods, though, the change would create problems because the cell addresses in the copied functions would no longer refer to the proper cells. This would result in an error message, ERR, being placed in the cell where the function contained the incorrect cell reference.

To illustrate this, try copying the formula in C23 to C24.

1. Press `Ctrl`-`C`

2. Press `Enter` to accept the block.

3. When prompted for the destination block, move to C24, and press `Enter`

The formula is copied, but the ERR message appears. Move back to C24 and look at the input line to see why. The copied formula reads @PMT(G6,C21,C22). Since C21 contains the value 48, Quattro Pro interprets it

Lesson 5/ More About Functions **57**

as the value to use for the interest rate. (Imagine a monthly interest rate of 48%!) C22 is blank, so Quattro Pro cannot calculate the result. Press (Del) to delete the incorrect formula.

Before it can be copied, then, the formula in C23 must be edited so that the cell addresses for interest and payment periods, C20 and C21, are absolute, rather than relative. That way the formula will always refer to those two cells, even when it is copied. To change the cell reference to absolute,

1. Move to C23.

2. Press (F2) to edit it.

3. Move the cursor until it is on the second cell address, C20.

4. Press (F4)

   $s will be inserted, and the cell address will now read C20.

5. Move the cursor to the next cell address in the formula, C21.

6. Press (F4)

   Again, $s will be inserted, so the cell address will now read C21.

7. Press (Enter) to enter the changes.

   Notice that the displayed value, $357.40, does not change.

Now you can copy the formulas in E23 and G23 to calculate monthly payments easily for all the cars. Move to C23 if you are not there already, and press (Ctrl)-(C). You are prompted for the source block of cells. Use (→) to extend the block through G23, and press (Enter).

Next, you are prompted for the destination. Since you want to calculate the monthly payments for the eight remaining cars, you need to specify a block eight rows deep. To do this,

1. Move to C24, and type a period to anchor the block. Extend the block through C31.

2. Press (Enter)

3. The formulas are copied. Some of the values are too large to be displayed in column C, however. Use (Ctrl)-(W) to change the width of the column to 12.

   The bottom part of the spreadsheet will look like Figure 5-3 on the following page.

As you can see, for as little as $295.78 or as much as $6778.28 per month, that classic car you covet can be yours.

The copy command shows the advantage of using cell addresses to display the make and model of each car. If the labels were retyped or copied as labels, each one would have to be retyped or recopied. Instead, the single copy command re-created the entire list.

This spreadsheet, like all others, will rapidly recalculate formulas when

Figure 5-3
@PMT function

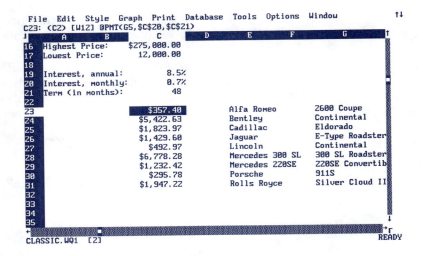

values are changed. To see this feature in action, assume that you can find an interest rate of 7.5% rather than 8.5%.

1. Move to cell C19.
2. Press F2, edit the annual interest rate to read 0.075, and press Enter

The monthly payments for all cars are automatically recalculated.

SOLVE FOR

The method of developing formulas and copying them works well if you have a limited number of specific options to analyze. In many cases, though, the choices are not as clear-cut. The question you wish to ask may not be "What are the monthly payments for this car?" but "Since I can afford up to a certain amount for monthly payments, what price range should I be looking in?" For that question, you can use Solve For, a special feature on Quattro Pro's /Tools menu, which lets you work backward from the desired result of a formula to the conditions needed to produce that result. You must let Quattro Pro know the Target Value, the desired result of the formula—in this case the monthly payments you would like to pay. You must also tell Quattro Pro the Formula Cell, where the formula (in this case, the @PMT function) is located, and the Variable Cell, where the result of Solve For (in this case the loan principal) should be placed.

Assume, then, that you have decided that you would like the monthly payments for your classic car to remain under $500 per month. Your Target Value is therefore 500. You must also set up a Formula Cell and a Variable Cell. The formula must include the Variable Cell in the appropriate place in the formula. Follow these steps to set up the Formula and Variable Cells:

1. Enter the following labels in cells A33 and A34:

   A

   33 **Desired payment:**

   34 **Highest principal:**

   "Desired payment" is the label for the Formula Cell, to be placed in C33, and "Highest principal" is the label for the Variable Cell, to be placed in C34.

2. Enter the formula **@PMT(C34,C20,C21)** in C33 by copying it from cell C31, and use F2 to edit it to C34 for the principal.

3. Move to C34, and use Ctrl-F to format it for currency, with two decimal places. You can format it even though there is no value in it yet; that way, when the result is calculated, it will be displayed as currency.

You are now ready to use **S**olve For to calculate the result, to be placed in C34.

1. Select /**T**ools¦**S**olve For

   A pop-up menu appears (refer to Figure 5-4).

Figure 5-4
Solve For menu

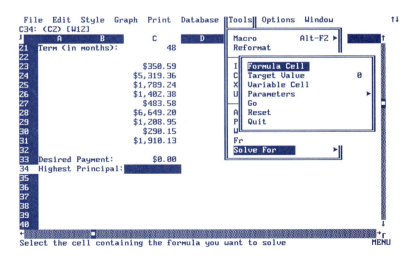

60   First Look at Quattro Pro 2.0/3.0

2. Select **Formula** Cell.

   The input line reads: "Formula Cell: C34".

3. Move to C33, the cell containing the formula. Press ⌷Enter⌷. (You could also have typed the cell address and then pressed ⌷Enter⌷.) You are returned to the Solve For menu.

4. Select **Target** Value. You are prompted for the Target Value, in this case the monthly payment you wish to make.

5. Type **500** and press ⌷Enter⌷

   Again, you are returned to the menu.

6. Select **Variable** Cell.

   The input line reads: "Variable Cell: C34".

7. Since the Variable cell is C34, press ⌷Enter⌷ to accept it.

You have now specified the necessary information. To calculate the result,

1. Select **Go**.

2. Select **Quit** (or press ⌷Esc⌷ to remove the menu from the screen).

The result has been calculated: Given a monthly payment of no more than $500, a loan term of 4 years, and an annual interest rate of 7.5%, the highest loan principal you could obtain is $20,679.19. You can now peruse the classic car advertisements, concentrating on cars costing less than $20,600, since you know they will fit your budget.

If this seems too limiting, you can try extending the term of the loan. Imagine your loan is for 10 years, not 4. The number of payment periods would then be 120.

1. Move to C21 .

2. Type **120** and press ⌷Enter⌷

Notice that although the monthly payments in cells C23 through C31 have been recalculated, the Highest Principal amount in C34 has not. To recalculate a value produced by **Solve** For, you must use **Solve** For again.

1. Select /**Tools** ¦**Solve** For.

The Formula Cell, Target Value, and Variable Cell values have all been retained from your last calculation. Since you do not need to change anything,

2. Select **Go**. The Highest Principal is recalculated to $42,122.37 (see Figure 5-5).

To remove all existing values from **Solve** For, use **Reset**.

1. Select **Reset**.

2. Select **Quit** to leave the Solve For menu.

Lesson 5/ More About Functions   **61**

Figure 5-5
Recalculation using Solve For

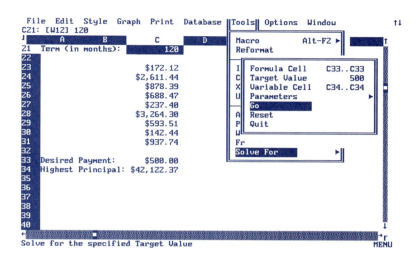

USING THE @IF FUNCTION

The last function you will use is the @IF function, which allows you to set up a condition. If the condition is met, Quattro Pro will insert a specified value, label, or formula. If it is not met, Quattro Pro will insert a different value, label, or formula. The function has the structure @IF(condition, what to do if condition is met, what to do if not met).

Assume that you feel it is too difficult to look over the list of car payments and decide which ones are less than your desired payment. You can use @IF to set up a condition: If the car payment on the list is less than the desired payment, YES will be entered. If it is more, NO will be entered. To see how this feature works, start by entering the function for the first car on the list, the Alfa Romeo 2600 Coupe.

1. Move to A23.
2. Press [Alt]-[F3] to bring up the Function menu.
3. Select IF.
4. Move to the first car payment at C23.
5. Type < (less than).
6. Move to the desired payment, C33.
7. Press [F4] to make it an absolute cell reference.
8. Type ,
9. Type **"YES"**

10. Type ,

11. Type **"NO"**

12. Type **)**

13. Press [Enter] to enter the formula.

YES appears in A23.

Look at the formula on the input line:

"@IF(C23<C33,"YES","NO")"

It says that if the value in C23 is less than the value in C33, YES should be entered into the cell. If not, NO should be entered. C23 is a relative cell reference, whereas C33 is an absolute cell reference, so that the formula can easily be copied for all the monthly payments on the list. The quotation marks around "YES" and "NO" in the formula are to let Quattro Pro know you are typing a word, not a cell reference. They do not appear in the cell, as you can see.

Copy the formula in A23 to A24..A31. When you are done, the bottom of the spreadsheet should look like Figure 5-6.

Figure 5-6
@IF function

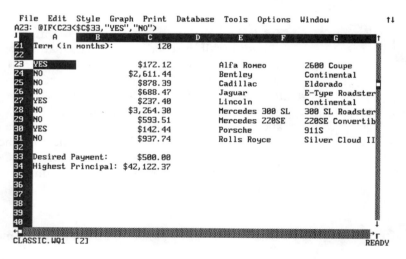

You have now completed the Classic Car spreadsheet. Press [Ctrl]-[S] and save the spreadsheet as CLASSIC.WQ1. Then, press [Ctrl]-[X] to leave Quattro Pro.

■ SUMMARY OF COMMANDS

Topic or Feature	Command or Reference	Menu	Page
Change Alignment	[Ctrl]-[A]	/Style | Alignment	51

Lesson 5 / More About Functions   **63**

Topic or Feature	Command or Reference	Menu	Page
Conditional Statement	@IF		61
Comma Format	Ctrl–F , ,	/Style ¦ Numeric Format ¦	52
Count	@COUNT		52
Enter All Capital Letters	Caps Lock		49
Linking Cells	+, cell address		55
Loan Payments	@PMT		54
Percentage Format	Ctrl–F , P	/Style ¦ Numeric Format ¦ Percentage	55
Maximum Value	@MAX		52
Minimum Value	@MIN		52
Quit a Menu		Quit on menu	50
Quit a Menu	Esc		60
Reset Solve for Values	Reset	/Tools ¦ Solve For ¦ Reset	60
Solve for a Target Amount	Solve For	/Tools ¦ Solve For	58

■ *SELF-TEST*

1. What steps would you follow to right-align cell contents? _____

   _____

   _____ .

2. The _____ function is used to calculate the number of items in a block.

3. The _____ function is used to calculate the highest value in a block.

4. The _____ function is used to calculate the lowest value in a block.

5. The _____ function is used to calculate loan payments.

6. What information must be included in the function in Question 5? _____

   _____ .

64 First Look at Quattro Pro 2.0/3.0

7. Press _____ to insert $s into an absolute cell address in a function without typing them.

8. You are at cell A14. What would you enter to create a link with the value in A1 so that if A1 changed, A14 would change as well? _____
_____ .

9. Use the _____ feature to work backward from the desired result of a formula.

10. What three pieces of information must you give Quattro Pro before executing the command in Question 6? _____
_____
_____
_____ .

11. In cell B1, you have entered the formula +(C1*.06)*12. The formula represents the price of widgets (C1) with 6% sales tax, sold in packs of 12. You would like to sell the 12-packs for $48. What steps would you follow to

have Quattro Pro calculate the value in C1? _____
_____
_____ .

12. To enter a conditional statement, use the _____ function.

13. What three pieces of information must you include in the function in Question 12? _____
_____
_____
_____ .

# Setting Up a Database

OBJECTIVES

At the end of this lesson, you will be able to:

- Design a database in Quattro Pro.
- Fill a block with sequential values.
- Assign names to database fields, which can be used in database operations.
- Sort a database.
- Set up search criteria to find specific records.
- Locate database records that meet specific criteria.
- Extract database records that meet specific criteria and copy them to a new section of the spreadsheet.

DESIGNING A DATABASE

For many spreadsheet applications, you can analyze data simply by organizing them into rows and columns. But in some cases you will need other kinds of tools to manipulate data. You may have to sort them according to the information in specific columns or search through to find data that fit certain criteria. For these situations, you must set up your data as a database, a collection of information organized into fields (also called variables) and records. The most common example of a database is a personal address book. Each person or company in it—each separate entry—is a **record**. Each piece of information in the record—name, address, telephone number—is a **field**. Most address books are organized according to the last names or company names of the entries. In "database talk," most address databases are sorted on the key field of last or company name. An ordinary address book can be arranged in only one order (sorted on one key field), unless you cut it apart and rearrange it. The same addresses, when placed in a database on a computer, can be sorted on last name, first name, ZIP code, street address, or whatever field you specify. The computer can also search for a specified name or find all entries with a specified area code much more quickly than you can.

Many computer programs are designed specifically to handle databases. Although Quattro Pro is not a pure database program, it includes some of the most useful features of a database, together with its powerful spreadsheet capabilities. You can define records and fields, sort on key fields, and search for records where certain fields meet certain criteria.

In designing a database, you must keep in mind how Quattro Pro expects records and fields to be entered. Each *record* should fit on one row, with each *field* placed in a separate column of that row. For example, if you want to enter the information from your personal address book into a Quattro Pro database, you enter the name, address, and telephone number all on the same row, rather than on separate rows as they might be in your address book. "Last Name" might be one field, and all last names have to be entered in the same column, for example, column A. All first names can be entered in column B, all street addresses in column C, all cities in D, all states in E, all countries in F, and all telephone numbers in G. You can then assign names to each column and refer to those names when sorting or searching the database. The advantage of using Quattro Pro rather than a database program is that the cells and columns can still be manipulated and used in spreadsheet calculations as usual. You can still use the editing and analysis tools you learned in previous lessons.

To illustrate this feature, you will create an application using a database based on the sales records of a video store. Assume that information on each video in stock—including title, price, and unit sales (updated monthly)—used to be kept on index cards. Sales have grown to the point that you, as store manager, want a more efficient way of keeping track of them than crossing out the old unit sales figures and writing in the new ones each month. You would also like to quickly calculate total sales, sort records, and search through records without having to shuffle many boxes of index cards. Therefore, you decide to enter the information into a Quattro Pro database.

Setting up a database requires careful planning. Follow these instructions and refer to Figure 6-1 to enter the data for the application.

Figure 6-1
Video spreadsheet

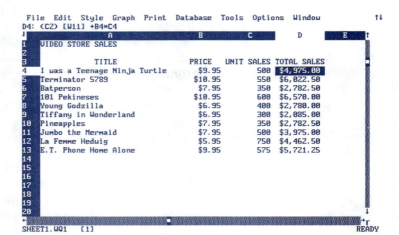

Lesson 6/Setting Up a Database   **67**

1. Since each column must contain a separate field of the database, you should make columns wide enough to hold each field. The fields will be TITLE, PRICE, UNIT SALES, and TOTAL SALES. Use Ctrl-W or /Style¦Column Width to expand columns A through D to the following widths:

Column	Width
A	30
B	11
C	11
D	11

2. For the title of the spreadsheet, move to A1, type **VIDEO STORE SALES** and press Enter

3. In cells A3 through D3, enter the labels for the database fields:

Cell	Label
A3	**TITLE**
B3	**PRICE**
C3	**UNIT SALES**
D3	**TOTAL SALES**

4. Use Ctrl-A or /Style¦Alignment to align the titles in the **C**enter of the cells A3 through D3.

5. In cells A4 through C13, enter the following data:

	A	**B**	**C**
4	**I Was a Teenage Ninja Turtle**	**9.95**	**500**
5	**Terminator 5789**	**10.95**	**550**
6	**Batperson**	**7.95**	**350**
7	**'101 Pekineses**	**10.95**	**600**
8	**Young Godzilla**	**6.95**	**400**
9	**Tiffany in Wonderland**	**6.95**	**300**
10	**Pineapples**	**7.95**	**350**
11	**Jumbo the Mermaid**	**7.95**	**500**
12	**La Femme Hedwig**	**5.95**	**750**
13	**E.T. Phone Home Alone**	**9.95**	**575**

6. Column D, TOTAL SALES, should contain PRICE multiplied by UNIT SALES.

68 First Look at Quattro Pro 2.0/3.0

(a) Move to D4 and enter the first formula for this.

(b) Type **+B4*C4** and press Enter

Then use Ctrl-C, or /Edit !Copy to copy the formula to cells D5 through D13. Use the technique for copying to many cells at once discussed in the last lesson.

7. Finally, use Ctrl-F or /Style !Numeric Format to display the values in the PRICE and TOTAL SALES columns, B4..B13 and D4..D13, in currency format.

The spreadsheet should look like Figure 6-1.

FILLING A BLOCK WITH SEQUENTIAL VALUES

The data entry for the database is complete. Before using the Quattro Pro commands to define it as a database, though, you should learn a useful editing technique called /Edit !Fill, which lets you fill a block with sequential values. It is especially useful in a database because it can be used to assign each record an identification number. Assume that you want to assign each record a number, starting with 1 for "I Was a Teenage Ninja Turtle." These identification numbers will be assigned to a new field, ID NUMBER. You will place the identification number in a column to the left of the video title.

Insert a new column to hold the field. To do this,

1. Place the highlight any-where on column A, and

(a) Press Ctrl-I (or /Edit !Insert).

(b) Select **C**olumn.

(c) Press Enter (to accept column block A).

2. Type the title.

(a) Move to A3.

(b) Type **ID NUMBER** and press Enter

3. You are now ready to fill cells A4 through A13 with sequential values, starting with 1. Select /Edit !Fill. The prompt is: "Destination for cells: A3".

Since you want the values to start at A4, press ↓. Type a period to anchor the cell block, and use ↓ to extend it to A13. Press Enter to accept the block.

4. A box appears, prompting you for the Start value, the first number of the sequence. This can be any number. Type **1** and press Enter.

5. Another box appears, prompting you for the Step value, the amount by which to increase each value. If you choose 1, the sequence will be 1, 2, 3,... If you choose 10, the sequence will be 1, 11, 21, ... Type **1** and press Enter.

6. A third box appears, prompting you for the Stop value, the value at which to end the sequence. If you don't specify a stop value, Quattro Pro will stop when it reaches either the default number, 8191, or the end of the specified block. Since you have specified a block of cells already and the number won't reach 8191, you need not specify a stop value. Just press Enter.

The cell block will be filled with sequential values (Figure 6-2).

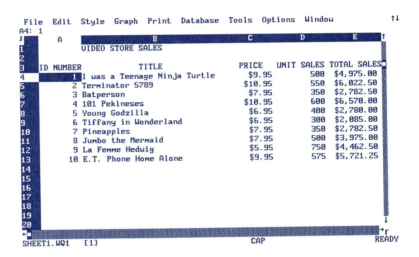

Figure 6-2
Adding sequential values

This technique is especially useful for entering a long sequence of order numbers. To demonstrate this, assume that the video data were entered in the order of the original purchase order numbers, which began at 12345. Select /Edit|Fill. Quattro Pro remembers the last block you specified, so you need not specify it again. Just press Enter. Enter the Start Value as 12345, the Step Value as 1, and the Stop Value as 50000. Again, the block will be filled with sequential values, starting at 12345.

· · · · · · · · · ·
ASSIGNING NAMES TO FIELDS

Now you are ready to assign names to your fields. You of course already know what the field names are: ID NUMBER, TITLE, PRICE, UNIT SALES,

70 First Look at Quattro Pro 2.0/3.0

and TOTAL SALES. But for Quattro Pro to recognize the names, you have to use the /Database¦Query¦Assign Names command. For this command to work, you must always set up your database as you did in this application: one record per row, each field in a separate row, and no lines or blank rows between the field names and field data.

To assign names to fields, first define the block that contains the database.

1. Move to A3.

2. Press (Shift)-(F7). Use the arrow keys to extend the block through E13.

3. Select /Database¦Query. This brings up the Query menu.

4. Type **B** (for **B**lock). The block is defined from A3 through E13.

5. Type **A** (for **A**ssign). The fields are assigned their respective names.

6. Type **Q** (for **Q**uit) to return to the spreadsheet.

··········
SORTING THE DATABASE

Assume you want to sort the videos in alphabetical order to make it easier for your staff to find information. As with other Quattro Pro commands, first specify the block containing the cells you want to sort, in this case the entire database. The block must include all rows and columns that make up the database, but it must *not* include the field titles.

1. Use (Shift)-(F7) to specify the block to be sorted, A4 through E13. (You can specify a block from any corner. Since you are already at E13, you may wish to press (Shift)-(F7) and extend the block backward to A4). Once the block is extended,select /Database¦Sort, which brings up the Sort menu. Type **B** (for **B**lock).

2. Next, specify the key field to sort on. Type **1** (for **1**st Key). The input line reads: "Column to be used as first sort key: A4".

3. Move to B4 and press (Enter)

   A window will appear prompting you for the sort order, A (Ascending) or D (Descending).

4. Type **A** and press (Enter)

Notice that the name of the field and the sort order are displayed on the sort menu to the right of 1st Key (Figure 6-3). If the displayed field is incorrect, you can correct it by choosing 1st Key again.

Figure 6-3
Sorting a database

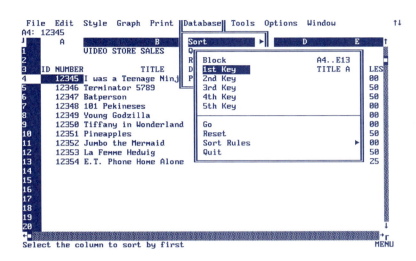

To sort the database, press **G** (for **G**o). The database is sorted in alphabetical order by title.

Although specifying the key field by choosing a column is very efficient in many cases, it can get cumbersome when working with large databases. If you were working with a large database extending over many columns, for example, it would be very inconvenient to move back through all the columns just to specify one as the key sort field. For that reason, Quattro Pro lets you use the field names when specifying a key. To illustrate this approach, select /**D**atabase|**S**ort.

The block is already defined. This time, though, assume you want to sort on TOTAL SALES, not TITLE.

1. Select **1**st Key.

2. Type **Total Sales** and press Enter. (You may use upper- or lowercase.)

3. When prompted for the sort order, type **A** and press Enter.

4. To perform the sort, select **G**o.

The data are now sorted in order of total sales.

Oh no! You've just realized that your only complete set of inventory records on index cards is in order of ID NUMBER. You have to be able to check each record in the computer database against its index card, but now that you've sorted it in alphabetical order, that's impossible to do. It would take weeks to alphabetize all those index cards so that they match the current form of the computer database. Fortunately, you have guarded against having to do this by including the ID number as one of the database fields, and so you can easily organize the computer database in order of ID NUMBER again. Do this

72 First Look at Quattro Pro 2.0/3.0

now, using /Database|Sort and specifying ID NUMBER as the key field. When you have finished, the database should, once again, be in order of ID NUMBER.

SEARCHING THROUGH YOUR DATA

Databases are shown to their best advantage when used to quickly find or extract data. To see how this feature works, assume that you want to find the videos for which total sales are less than $3,000 in order to make them part of a sales drive. You can do this by first setting up a criteria table—that is, a group of cells which sets the criteria for the search. In this case, the criterion is TOTAL SALES < 3000. You can then use either /Database|Query|Locate to search the database, locating those records that fit the criterion, or /Database|Query|Extract to place the information in a specially designated area called the **Output Block**.

1. Begin the process by setting up the criteria table. To label the criteria table, move to B15 and type **Criteria Table:** and press ⬇

2. Enter the field to use in the criteria, in this case TOTAL SALES. In the row just below it, place the criteria, in this case TOTAL SALES < 3000. Type **TOTAL SALES** and press ⬇

3. Finally, enter the search criterion: Type **+TOTAL SALES<3000** and press [Enter]

   The + is to let Quattro Pro know you are typing a formula.

The criteria table is now set up. You now must let Quattro Pro know where it is.

1. Select /Database|Query. This brings up the Query menu again. Notice that the block is still defined from the Assign Names command. Since you will use the same block in this command, you do not need to redefine it.

2. Type **C** (for **C**riteria Table).

   The input line reads: "Enter criterion block: B17".

Move the highlight to B16, type a period to anchor the block, and extend it through B17. Then press [Enter] to accept the block. You are returned to the /Database|Query menu.

To locate all records that meet the criterion,

1. Type **L** (for **L**ocate).

   Quattro Pro highlights the first record to match the criterion (Figure 6-4).

2. Press ⬇ to find the other records.

Figure 6-4
Locating database records

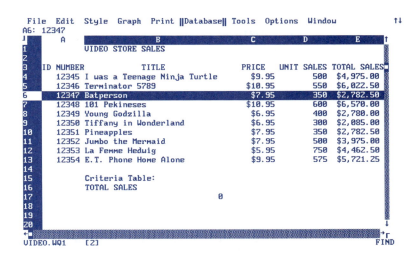

When you reach the end,

1. Press [Esc] to return to the /Database|Query menu.
2. Press [Esc] again to return to the spreadsheet.

EXTRACTING RECORDS FROM A DATABASE

Locating records that meet certain criteria can be useful, but for working with them in more detail, it is often easier to extract them and copy them to a separate part of the database, the output block. To extract records, you first set up a criteria table, as you did for /Database|Query|Locate. For this example, use the already-defined criteria table. Then you must set up the output block, the block of cells where you want the extracted data to go. You must also specify which fields you want included in the output block. Do this by typing the field names you want extracted in the columns where you want them to be placed. You must also let Quattro Pro know where the output block is by specifying it on the /Database|Query menu.

1. Move to B18.
2. Type **Output Block:** and press [↓]
3. At B19, type **TITLE** and press [→]
4. At C19, type **PRICE** and press [Enter]

Quattro Pro will place the title and price information of the videos that meet the search criterion directly underneath, starting at row 20.

74   First Look at Quattro Pro 2.0/3.0

> **CAUTION: Quattro Pro will overwrite any existing information, so be sure to place output blocks in a blank area of the spreadsheet.**

To specify the output block,

1. Select /**D**atabase ¦**Q**uery.

2. Type **O** (for **O**utput Block).

   The input line reads: "Enter block to copy to with Extract or Unique: C19".

Specify the top row of the block, the one containing the field names. In this case, the block extends from B19 to C19. To specify the block,

1. Move to B19, type a period, extend the block to C19, and press Enter.

To extract the records,

1. Press **E** (for **E**xtract).

2. Select **Q**uit to leave the /**D**atabase ¦**Q**uery menu.

The titles and prices of the videos that meet the criterion are listed in cells B20 through C23 (Figure 6-5).

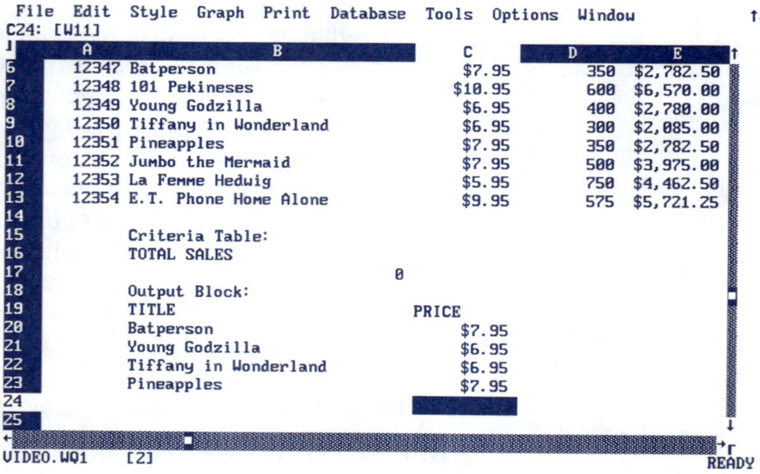

Figure 6-5

Extracting database records

```
 File  Edit  Style  Graph  Print  Database  Tools  Options  Window         ↑↓
 C24: [W11]
 ⌐         A               B                 C        D          E        ⌐
 6    12347 Batperson                       $7.95     350   $2,782.50
 7    12348 101 Pekineses                  $10.95     600   $6,570.00
 8    12349 Young Godzilla                  $6.95     400   $2,780.00
 9    12350 Tiffany in Wonderland          $6.95     300   $2,085.00
 10   12351 Pineapples                      $7.95     350   $2,782.50
 11   12352 Jumbo the Mermaid               $7.95     500   $3,975.00
 12   12353 La Femme Heduig                 $5.95     750   $4,462.50
 13   12354 E.T. Phone Home Alone           $9.95     575   $5,721.25
 14
 15         Criteria Table:
 16         TOTAL SALES
 17                                 0
 18         Output Block:
 19         TITLE                   PRICE
 20         Batperson               $7.95
 21         Young Godzilla          $6.95
 22         Tiffany in Wonderland   $6.95
 23         Pineapples              $7.95
 24
 25                                                                         ↓
 ←                  ▪                                                   →r
 VIDEO.WQ1   [2]                                                    READY
```

You have now been introduced to Quattro Pro's database features. Save the spreadsheet as VIDEO.WQ1, and exit Quattro Pro.

Lesson 6/ Setting Up a Database   **75**

■ *SUMMARY OF COMMANDS*

Topic or Feature	Command or Reference	Menu	Page
Assign Names to Database Fields	Assign Names	/Database ¦ Query ¦ Assign Names	70
Enter Sequential Values	Fill	/Edit ¦ Fill	68
Extract Records	Extract	/Database ¦ Query ¦ Extract	74
Locate Records	Locate	/Database ¦ Query ¦ Locate	72
Set up an Output Block	Output Block	/Database ¦ Query ¦ Output Block	73
Set up a Block to Sort	Sort	/Database ¦ Sort ¦ Block	70
Set up a Criteria Table	Criteria Table	/Database ¦ Query ¦ Criteria Table	72
Set up a Block to Query	Query	/Database ¦ Query ¦ Block	73
Set up a Sort Key	Sort	/Database ¦ Sort ¦ 1st Key	70
Sort a Database	Sort	/Database ¦ Sort ¦ Go	70

■ *SELF-TEST*

1. A database consists of information organized into _____ and _____ .

2. In a Quattro Pro database, each _____ must be entered in a separate column, and each _____ must be entered in a separate row.

3. Give an example of when it is useful to fill a block with sequential values.

   _____

   _____ .

First Look at Quattro Pro 2.0/3.0

4. What three pieces of information must you give Quattro Pro to fill a block with sequential values? _____

_____ .

5. What is the purpose of /Database ┊Query ┊Assign Names? _____

_____

_____ .

6. The column that Quattro Pro uses to sort a database in a given order is called a _____ .

7. When you select /Database ┊Sort ┊1st Key, you can specify the column in two ways. What are they? _____

_____ .

8. A spreadsheet block that specifies search criteria is called a(n) _____ .

9. List two commands from the /Database ┊Query menu that require a(n) [answer to Question 8] _____ .

10. A spreadsheet block that specifies where Quattro Pro should copy database information which fits specified criteria is called a(n)

_____ .

LESSON SEVEN · Creating Graphs

OBJECTIVES

At the end of this lesson, you will be able to:

- Create bar and line graphs.
- Specify X- and Y-axis series to use in creating the graph.
- Use F10 to view the current graph.
- Edit series by editing cell contents.
- Add series labels, graph titles, and interior labels.
- Save the graph by naming it.
- Display a named graph.
- Close a spreadsheet without leaving the program.

You've been working hard all week to get a spreadsheet report ready for your boss. You've arranged all the facts and figures in nice tidy columns, using lines and boxes to enhance the impact of the most important information. Friday morning, you go into the main office to deliver the report. The boss leafs through it, hands it back, and says, "Great job, but I'm too busy to go through all these figures. Tell you what. Why don't you draw me a picture of it? And get it back to me by Monday morning."

Fortunately, you've created the report using Quattro Pro, so you don't have to run down to the corner drugstore to pick up a ruler and compass and spend all weekend trying to "draw a picture" of your data. Instead, you can use Quattro Pro's graphing tools to create whatever kinds of charts you need. In this lesson, you will be introduced to Quattro Pro's basic graphing tools; in the next lesson, you will learn how to annotate your graphs.

CREATING A GRAPH

Suppose that your report involves creating a graph of classic car prices. Start Quattro Pro, if you have not already done so, and open the CLASSIC.WQ1 file. Press Home to move to A1 if you are not there already.

The first step in any graph is to decide what type of graph—bar, line, or

78   First Look at Quattro Pro 2.0/3.0

pie—you wish to create. Then, specify the blocks of data, or **series**, you wish to use to create it. The block used to define the values on the X-axis is called the **X-Series**; the blocks used to define the values on the Y-axis are called the **Y-Series**. You can include titles and legends to identify the series. You can display the graph at any point and change whatever features you wish. Finally, you can save the graph with the spreadsheet so that you have a permanent copy.

All these features are found on the /Graph menu. Select /**Graph** and look at the menu. The screen should look like Figure 7-1.

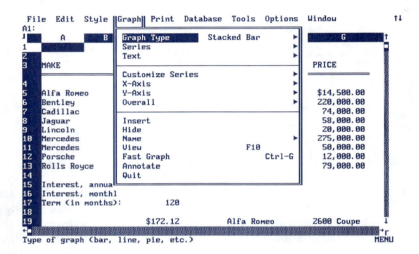

Figure 7-1
Graph menu

GRAPH TYPE

When you first select the /Graph menu, the Graph Type is set to Stacked Bar. To see the other Graph Types,

1. Type **G** (for **G**raph Type).

Figure 7-2 shows the possible graph types.

To choose a different graph type, you select the new type from the menu. For now, keep the graph type as Stacked Bar. Press [Esc] to return to the main /Graph menu.

SERIES

Once you have chosen a graph type, your next step is to specify the series for Quattro Pro to use in creating the graph. Quattro Pro creates a graph the same

Lesson 7 / Creating Graphs   **79**

Figure 7-2
Types of graphs

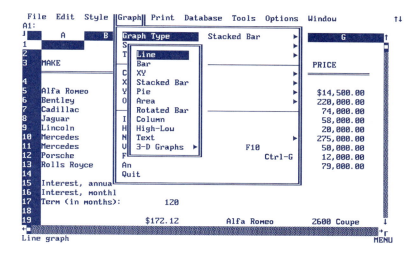

way you would, by plotting series of numbers on the X- and Y-axes. Assume that you want to use the car makes for the X-series and their respective prices for the Y-series. To specify these choices, select Series from the main /Graph menu.

> ***CAUTION: The /Graph menu contains three items relating to series: Series, X-Axis, and Y-Axis. Choose Series to specify the series; the other two choices include features for customizing the series once they have been specified.***

Type **S** (for **S**eries). The Series menu is displayed (Figure 7-3).

Figure 7-3
Series menu

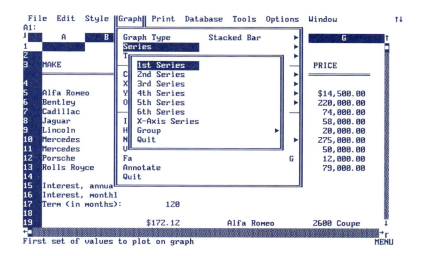

You can specify one X-axis series and up to six Y-axis series. In this case, you will specify only the first Y-axis series.

1. Press **1** (for **1**st Y-Series).

   The input line reads: "Enter 1st series block: A1".

You specify the block in what should now be a very familiar fashion.

1. Move the highlight to the first price in G5.
2. Type a period to anchor the block.
3. Press ↓ to extend the block to include all the prices, through G13.
4. Press Enter to accept the block. You will be returned to the /Graph¦Series menu.

Follow the same steps to specify the car makes for the X-series. From the /Graph¦Series menu,

1. Type **X** (for **X**-Series). The input line reads: "Enter X-axis labels block:".
2. Move the highlight to the first car make in A5.
3. Type a period to anchor the block.
4. Press ↓ to extend the block to include all the prices, through A13.
5. Press Enter to accept the block. You will be returned to the /Graph¦Series menu.
6. Type **Q** (for **Q**uit) to return to the main /Graph menu.

> **CAUTION:** *If you make a mistake while defining a single series, you can simply redefine that series by selecting it again from the /Graph¦Series menu. If you notice that you have made several mistakes and want to start over, select /Graph¦Customize Series¦Reset¦Graph, which will remove all series blocks you have specified.*

DISPLAYING THE GRAPH

You are now ready to display the graph. The menu selection for this is /Graph¦View; the shortcut key is F10. Press F10. The graph is displayed on the screen (Figure 7-4).

Figure 7-4
Bar graph, unedited labels

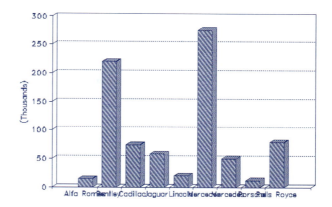

Quattro Pro has created a graph, but it is not a very elegant one. The titles on the X-axis run together so much that they are impossible to read. You could shorten the titles, but you really do want to display the car make on the graph. Perhaps the best idea would be to try another graph type.

To remove the graph from the screen and return to the menu or spreadsheet from which you started, you can press any key. Press (Esc). You are returned to the main /Graph menu.

1. Select **G**raph Type.

   Look at the list of graph types. How about trying Rotated Bar?

2. Type **R** (for **R**otated Bar). The Graph Type on the /Graph menu has been changed to Rotated Bar.

3. Press (F10).

   The new graph is displayed (Figure 7-5).

Figure 7-5
Rotated bar graph

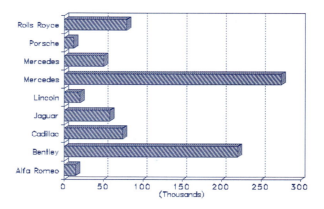

82   First Look at Quattro Pro 2.0/3.0

That's better. The car makes are now clearly displayed.

As you look at the graph, you may notice other features that could use some improvement. For one thing, there is no way to distinguish between the two types of Mercedes. Nor is it clear what the label (Thousands) refer to. And wouldn't a title be a useful addition? To make these changes, first return to the spreadsheet. Press Esc twice to return to the spreadsheet.

EDITING SERIES

The simplest way to clarify the difference between the two Mercedes is to edit the car make.

1. Move to A10.

2. Press F2, and edit the car make to read Mercedes 300SL.

3. Press ↓ to move to A11.

4. Press F2, edit the car make to read Mercedes 220SE, and press Enter. Since you have made changes in cells that are part of the X-series block, Quattro Pro automatically updates the graph to reflect those changes.

5. Press F10

As you can see on the monitor, the graph has been changed to reflect the changes in the X-series. Press Esc to return to the spreadsheet.

ADDING TEXT

To add text, including titles, to the graph, use /Graph ¦ Text.

1. Select /Graph.

2. Type **T** (for **T**ext).

The Text menu is displayed (Figure 7-6).

To give the graph a title,

1. Type **1** (for **1**st line of the Title).

A window appears with the prompt: "First Title Line:".

2. Type **CLASSIC CAR PRICES** and press Enter

The title will appear on the Text menu.

Figure 7-6
Text menu

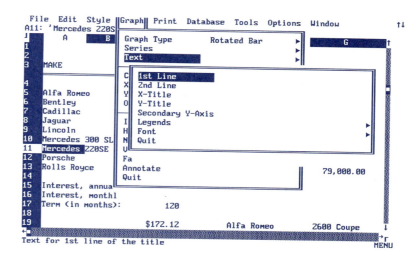

Next, to select the Y-axis title,

1. Type **Y** (for **Y**-Title). A window appears with the prompt: "Y-axis Title Line:".

2. Type **US DOLLARS** and press Enter

If you want to add a second title line or an X-axis title, choose the appropriate menu items.

Press F10 to display the graph (Figure 7-7). When you are finished looking at the graph, press Esc twice to return to the main /**G**raph menu. If you want to make additional changes to the graph, do so now.

Figure 7-7
Classic graph, edited labels

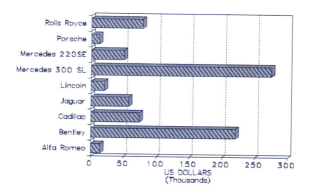

84 First Look at Quattro Pro 2.0/3.0

SAVING A GRAPH

Having developed a graph, you are now ready to save it. You do so by selecting **Name** from the /**Graph** menu and giving the graph a name. From the /**Graph** menu,

1. Type **N** (for **Name**).

   A menu with the following choices is displayed:

   Display

   Create

   Erase

   Reset

   Slide

   Graph Copy

NOTE: If you are using Quattro Pro 3.0, an additional choice, Autosave Edits, will be included on the menu.

2. Type **C** (for **Create**).

   A window appears with the prompt: "Enter graph name:".

3. Type **CLASSIC** and press (Enter)

The graph is saved with the name CLASSIC, and you are returned to the main /**Graph** menu.

DISPLAYING A NAMED GRAPH

To make sure that the graph has been saved correctly, you can display it. From the main /**Graph** menu,

1. Type **N** (for **Name**).

2. Type **D** (for **Display**).

A window appears prompting you for the name of the graph to display. To accept CLASSIC, press (Enter). Quattro Pro will display the graph you have just created. To return to the spreadsheet, press (Esc) twice.

You have completed the creation of a graph using the CLASSIC.WQ1 spreadsheet. The new graph you made has changed the spreadsheet; to save

Lesson 7 / Creating Graphs   **85**

the graph, you must save the spreadsheet. Press $\boxed{\text{Ctrl}}$-$\boxed{\text{S}}$, and select **R**eplace to save the spreadsheet with the changes.

CLOSING A SPREADSHEET

To continue working with graphs, you should close this spreadsheet and open a new one. Up to this point, whenever you saved a spreadsheet you immediately exited Quattro Pro. It is very inefficient, however, to have to exit Quattro Pro whenever you want to work on a new spreadsheet! For that reason, Quattro Pro provides the /**File**|**Close** command so that you can close a spreadsheet without leaving the program.

1. Select /**File**|**Close**. CLASSIC.WQ1 is removed from the screen, leaving SHEET1.WQ1. Now, open VIDEO to create a new graph.

2. Select /**File**|**O**pen, and choose VIDEO.WQ1.

3. Press $\boxed{\text{Home}}$ to move to A1 if you are not there already.

This time you will create a different kind of graph. Instead of just developing a bar chart, suppose you want to plot the relationship between video price and unit sales. If there were a relationship, it might affect future pricing of videos. For this kind of situation, a line graph is useful. PRICE values are used for the X-axis; UNIT SALES are used for the Y-axis.

Before you can create the graph, though, you must look at the way the data are currently displayed. The videos are arranged according to ID NUMBER rather than price. In your graph, however, you want to find out what happens to unit sales as prices go up. For Quattro Pro to graph that information properly, the database must be arranged in order of price; that is, it must be sorted on the key field PRICE. The first step, therefore, as in many graphs, is to arrange your data in the way that makes most sense for the project you are working on.

You learned in the last lesson how to arrange the data in a particular order. Simply select /**D**atabase|**S**ort, specify the block to be sorted, and select PRICE as the sort key.

1. Select /**D**atabase|**S**ort.

2. Select **B**lock.

3. Move the highlight to A4, type a period to anchor the block, use the arrow keys to extend it through E13, and press $\boxed{\text{Enter}}$ to accept the block. You are returned to the /**D**atabase|**S**ort menu.

4. Select **1**st Key.

5. Type **Price** and press Enter
6. Type **A** and press Enter
7. Select **Go**.

The database is sorted in order of price.

Now, use the following steps to create a line graph of video price and unit sales.

1. To specify Graph Type, select **/Graph ¦ Graph Type ¦ Line**.
2. To specify X-axis series, from the **/Graph** menu select **Series ¦ X-axis**, and specify the block C4..C13.
3. To specify Y-axis series, from the **/Graph ¦ Series** menu
    (a) Select **1st Series**, and specify the block D4..D13.
    (b) Select **Quit** to return to the main **/Graph** menu.
4. To specify titles, from the main **/Graph** menu
    (a) Select **Text ¦ 1st line**.
    (b) Type **VIDEO SALES** and press Enter
    (c) Select **X-Title**.
    (d) Type **PRICES** and press Enter
    (e) Select **Y-Title**.
    (f) Type **UNIT SALES** and press Enter
5. To display the graph (Figure 7-8), press F10

Figure 7-8
Videos graph

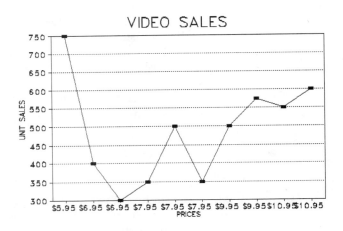

The graph shows some relationship between price and unit sales; overall, as prices go up, so do sales. The most likely explanation for this is that, within

Lesson 7/ Creating Graphs **87**

limits, sales are determined by a video's popularity, not just its price. The lowest-price video has the highest sales, though, and there is fluctuation within each price range. As store manager, you might want to consider having a special sale on the videos in each price range that are not selling very well.

ADDING INTERIOR LABELS

One problem with the graph you just created is that you can't tell the videos apart by looking at it. To do that, you have to add the video names as interior labels. The Interior Labels feature is on the /Graph ¦ Customize Series menu.

1. Press Esc twice to return to the main /Graph menu.

2. Type **C** (for **C**ustomize Series).

3. Type **I** (for **I**nterior Labels).

4. The Interior Labels menu gives you a choice of labeling the first through sixth Y-axis series. Since you only have one Y-axis series, type **1** (for **1**st Series).

   The input line reads: "Spreadsheet data to label the series:".

5. Move the highlight to the first video title at B4, type a period to anchor the block, use ⬇ to extend the block through B13, and press Enter to accept the block.

6. A window appears with choices for the position of the labels. Start out by selecting Below.

   (a) Type **B** (for **B**elow).

   (b) Press F10 to display the graph.

The labels are there, but they are not very attractive since many run together. Would a different label position help?

1. Press Esc to return to the /Graph ¦ Customize Series ¦ Interior Labels menu.

2. Select **1**st Series.

3. You are again prompted for a block. Since you wish to use the same block, press Enter

4. When the Interior Labels position menu appears,

   (a) Type **R** (for **R**ight).

(b) Press F10 to display the graph.

This is better, but not much.

EDITING LABELS

One way to improve the appearance of a graph is to selectively edit the labels, as you did with the two Mercedes labels in the last graph. In this case, you really need labels only for the videos in each price range with lower sales. Those videos are:

Tiffany in Wonderland

Pineapples

Batperson

I Was a Teenage Ninja Turtle

Terminator 5789

Since those are the only labels you want to display, you could erase all the others from the block you use to specify interior labels. Quattro Pro will interpret the blank cell as a blank label. Of course, you do not want to erase the titles from the database itself! Instead, you can copy the titles to a new block of cells, erase the ones you don't need, and specify the new block as the block to use for interior labels. Follow these directions:

1. Press Esc three times to return to the spreadsheet.

2. Copy the video titles from B4..B13 to G4..G13:

    (a) Move to B4, press Shift-F7, and extend the block to B13.

    (b) Press Ctrl-C

    (c) Move to G4, and press Enter. The labels are copied, and the highlight returns to B13.

3. Now, edit the new labels.

    (a) Move to G4.

    (b) Delete the following videos by placing the highlight on the cell and pressing Del:

    La Femme Hedwig

    Young Godzilla

    Jumbo the Mermaid

    E.T. Phone Home Alone

    101 Pekineses

Lesson 7/ Creating Graphs **89**

4. Next, specify G4..G13 as the block to use for interior labels:
   (a) Select **/G**raph **|C**ustomize Series **|I**nterior Labels.
   (b) Select **1**st Series.
5. Quattro Pro assumes you still wish to use block B4..B13. Since you do not, press [Esc]
6. Move the highlight to G4, type a period to anchor the block, extend it through G13, and press [Enter] to accept the new block.
7. Select **A**bove for the interior label position.
8. Finally, press [F10] to display the graph (Figure 7-9).

Figure 7-9
Interior labels, edited

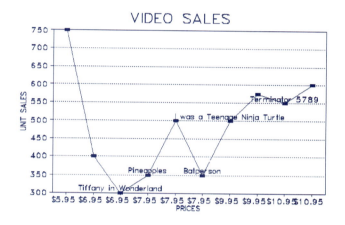

The graph displays the videos in each price range with the lowest sales. It would be improved if that information were included somewhere on the graph. Why not add POOREST-SELLING VIDEOS IN PRICE RANGE to the second line of the title?

10. Press [Esc] three times to return to the main **/G**raph menu.

ADDING A SECOND LINE TO THE TITLE

To add a second line to a title,

1. Select **T**ext from the main **/G**raph menu. The Text menu appears (refer to Figure 7-6 if necessary).

90 First Look at Quattro Pro 2.0/3.0

2. Type **2** (for **2**nd Line).

3. Type **POOREST-SELLING VIDEOS IN PRICE RANGE** and press ⌷Enter⌷

4. Press ⌷F10⌷ to display the graph.

You have now completed the graphs and will be able to present them to your boss on Monday without working all weekend. Before leaving Quattro Pro, be sure to save the graph with the name VIDEOS.

1. Press ⌷Esc⌷ twice to return to the main /Graph menu.

2. Select **N**ame ⌷**C**reate, and name the graph VIDEOS.

3. Select **Q**uit to return to the spreadsheet.

If you would like to print the graph, refer to the section on printing a graph in Lesson Ten. When you are finished, save the spreadsheet with the changes (press ⌷Ctrl⌷-⌷S⌷, and choose **R**eplace), and exit Quattro Pro.

■ SUMMARY OF COMMANDS

Topic or Feature	Command or Reference	Menu	Page
Close a Spreadsheet	Close	/File ⌷Close	85
Create a Graph	Graph	/Graph	78
Display a Named Graph	Graph Name	/Graph ⌷Name ⌷ Display	84
Graph Title	Graph Text	/Graph ⌷Text ⌷ 1–2	89
Graph Type	Graph Type	/Graph ⌷ Graph Type	78
Interior Labels	Customize Series	/Graph ⌷ Customize Series ⌷ Interior Labels	87
Save a Graph	Graph Name	/Graph ⌷Name ⌷ Create	84
View the Current Graph	⌷F10⌷	/Graph ⌷View	81
X-Axis Titles	Graph Text	/Graph ⌷Text ⌷ X-Axis Title	83
X-Axis Values	Series	/Graph ⌷Series ⌷ X-Series	80

Topic or Feature	Command or Reference	Menu	Page
Y-Axis Titles	Graph Text	/Graph ¦Text ¦ Y-Axis Title	83
Y-Axis Values	Series	/Graph ¦Series ¦ 1–6	80

■ *SELF-TEST*

1. List three types of Quattro Pro graphs you have used. _____ _____ .

2. A_____ is a list of values or labels Quattro Pro uses in creating graphs.

3. How many series can you specify for the Y-axis of a graph? _____ _____ .

4. How many series can you specify for the X-axis of a graph? _____ _____ .

5. Press _____ to display the current graph.

6. List three features you have used from the /Graph ¦Text menu. _____ _____ _____ _____ .

7. What menu is the Interior Labels feature on? _____ .

8. Use _____ to save a graph.

9. What happens to the current graph if you exit Quattro Pro without saving it and without saving changes to the spreadsheet? _____ _____ _____ .

LESSON EIGHT Annotating Graphs

OBJECTIVES

At the end of this lesson, you will be able to:

- Create a pie graph.
- Retrieve a file.
- Reset all graph settings.
- Remove grid lines from graphs.
- Display the Annotator screen.
- Recognize the parts of the Annotator.
- Create text boxes.
- Draw arrows.
- Exit the Annotator.
- Save changes to a graph.

CREATING A PIE GRAPH

In many cases, titles and labels are all you really need to create clear graphs. Imagine, for example, that you want to create a graph showing market share for your company and your closest competitor. You made 5479 widgets in the past year, and your competitor made 200. The easiest way to present this information is in a pie graph. Using a blank spreadsheet, follow these directions to create the graph.

1. Enter these data:

	A	B
1	US	5479
2	THEM	200

2. Select /Graph ¦Graph Type ¦Pie.

3. Select **S**eries ⁞ **X**-Axis Series, and specify block A1..A2.
4. Select **1**st Series, and specify block B1..B2.

   Then, select **Q**uit to return to the main /**G**raph menu
5. Select **T**ext ⁞ **1**st Line, type **MARKET SHARE FOR WIDGETS**, and press [Enter]
6. Press [Esc] twice to return to the spreadsheet.
7. Press [F10]

The graph will look like Figure 8-1. This graph really says it all. You don't need to add any other information. Press [Esc] to return to the spreadsheet.

Figure 8-1
Pie graph

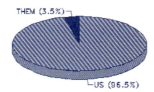

Save the graph with the name PIECHART.

1. Select /**G**raph ⁞ **N**ame ⁞ **C**reate, and specify PIECHART.
2. Press [Esc] to return to the spreadsheet.

Use [Ctrl]-[S] to save the spreadsheet with the name CHART.WQ1.

REASONS FOR ANNOTATING A GRAPH

Some graphs are more complicated than the one you just created and need additional text or illustration. For that contingency, Quattro Pro provides an Annotator, which lets you add comments and arrows or other graphics to enhance your graph. To demonstrate how to use the Annotator, you will use VIDEO.WQ1 and create a new graph, plotting PRICE against TOTAL SALES. Then you will use the Annotator to add text boxes and arrows.

94 First Look at Quattro Pro 2.0/3.0

RETRIEVING A FILE

At this point, you would like to leave CHART.WQ1 and bring up VIDEO.WQ1. You could do this by using /File ¦Close to close CHART.WQ1 and /File ¦Open to open VIDEOS.WQ1. However, Quattro Pro gives you a command, /File ¦Retrieve, that does both at once.

1. Select /File ¦Retrieve.

   You are prompted for a file, as you are when using the /File ¦Open command.

2. Select VIDEO.WQ1.

   CHART.WQ1 will be closed, and VIDEO.WQ1 will be displayed on the screen.

GRAPH RESET

When last you left VIDEO.WQ1, you had just created the VIDEOS graph. Quattro Pro saved all the settings just as you created them. To see the settings,

1. Select /Graph. As you can see, the graph type is still set for Line.

2. Select Series to see the series settings. The first Y-series is still set for D4..D13; the X-Axis series is still set for C4..C13.

3. To see the text.

   (a) Press (Esc)

   (b) Select Text.

The titles are still set. To return to the main /Graph menu, press (Esc). To see the graph, press (F10). As you can see, it is exactly the same as you left it. When you are done, press (Esc).

Quattro Pro saves your settings in case you want to make a number of graphs, each with the same heading or using the same series. In this case, though, you want to make an entirely new graph. You could change or delete each series and title individually, but Quattro Pro provides the /Graph ¦ Customize Series ¦Reset ¦Graph command to reset all graph settings to their default (original) values. The command will not affect any graph that you saved with a name. To reset the settings, from the main /Graph menu,

1. Select Customize Series.

2. Select Reset.

   The Reset menu appears (Figure 8-2).

Figure 8-2
Reset graph settings

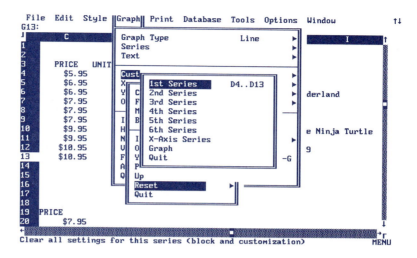

3. You can choose to reset individual series, leaving other series and titles alone, or reset the entire graph. Since you want to reset the entire graph, select **G**raph.

   All graph settings are returned to their original value.

4. Select **Q**uit to return to the /**G**raph menu.

   Note that the Graph Type has returned to the default, Stacked Bar. To verify that there are no graph settings, press F10.

   If graph settings were still in effect, a graph would be displayed. Since the /**G**raph menu has been reset, you will hear a bell and see a blank screen with the error message: "No series selected".

5. To return to the main /**G**raph menu, press Esc.

You are now ready to create a new graph, one that plots PRICE against TOTAL SALES. From the main /**G**raph menu, use the following steps to create the graph.

1. Select **G**raph **T**ype ¦**L**ine.

2. Select **S**eries.

3. Select **X**-Axis, and specify C4..C13.

4. Select **1**st Series, and specify E4..E13.

5. Select **Q**uit to return to the main /**G**raph menu.

6. Select **C**ustomize Series ¦**I**nterior Labels ¦**1**st Series, and specify B4..B13.

7. Select **A**bove.

8. Select **Q**uit to return to the Customize Series menu.

9. Select **Q**uit to return to the main /Graph menu.//
10. Select **T**ext.
11. Select **1**st Line, and type **SHOULD WE RAISE VIDEO PRICES?** Press [Enter]
12. Select **X**-Axis, type **PRICES**, and press [Enter]
13. Select **Y**-Axis, type **TOTAL SALES (U.S. DOLLARS)**, and press [Enter]
14. Select **Q**uit to return to the main /Graph menu.
15. Press [F10] to display the graph (Figure 8-3).

Figure 8-3
Total sales graph

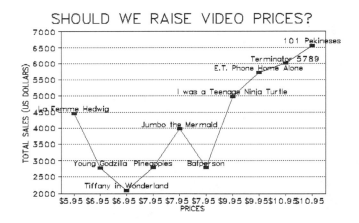

As the graph shows, the highest-priced videos have the highest total sales. If video sales really do depend more on popularity than price, maybe prices should be higher for the most popular videos. On the other hand, consider La Femme Hedwig. It is the lowest-priced video, and it has the highest unit sales, giving it a high total sales value. If the price were raised, would it make even more money for the store? Or would sales drop? How about the other videos in the $6.95 and $7.95 price range? Should the prices be raised, on the theory that the same number of people will continue to buy them? Or should they be lowered, in the hope that unit sales will increase dramatically, thus increasing total sales?

Unfortunately, Quattro Pro cannot make those decisions for you. It can, however, help you annotate the graph to present the questions clearly. You could clarify the issues and make the graph easier for other people to read by adding three text boxes, with arrows pointing to the appropriate videos. In the upper part of the graph you could add a box saying HIGHER–PRICED VIDEOS MAKE MORE MONEY FOR US, with an arrow pointing to the higher-priced videos. Below it, to the left, you could add another box with

Lesson 8/ Annotating Graphs   **97**

the text BUT THE LOWEST–PRICED VIDEO HAS THE HIGHEST UNIT SALES, and an arrow pointing to La Femme Hedwig. And in the lower right corner, you could add a third box with SHOULD MIDRANGE VIDEO PRICES BE RAISED OR LOWERED? and an arrow pointing to these videos.

REMOVING GRID LINES

But before returning to the /Graph menu to add the text boxes and arrows, take another look at the graph. Do you really need those grid lines? The sales figures would be clear without them, and they will make it harder to read the text boxes you intend to add. Why not get rid of them?

Press Esc to return to the main /Graph menu.

To get rid of grid lines,

1. Select **O**verall.

2. Select **G**rid. You will see the Grid menu, with the following choices:

   Horizontal

   Vertical

   Both

   Clear

   Grid Color

   Line Style

   Fill Color

   Quit

3. Select **C**lear.

4. Select **Q**uit to return to the main /Graph menu.

5. Press F10. The graph is displayed without the grid lines.

6. Press Esc to return to the main /Graph menu.

ANNOTATING A GRAPH

The graph is now ready to be annotated. Before doing so, however, it is a good idea to name the graph so that the settings are saved. If you make a mistake while annotating or decide you prefer the graph in its original form, you will have the original graph.

1. Select **Name** | **Create**.

   Since you already saved one graph with this spreadsheet, the graph name window will appear with the name of the existing graph, VIDEOS, highlighted.

2. Type **TOTAL SALES**, and press [Enter]

   The graph is saved with the new name, TOTAL SALES.

To annotate the graph,

1. From the main /**G**raph menu, select **A**nnotate.

   In a few seconds, the Annotator screen will appear (Figure 8-4).

Figure 8-4
Graph annotator

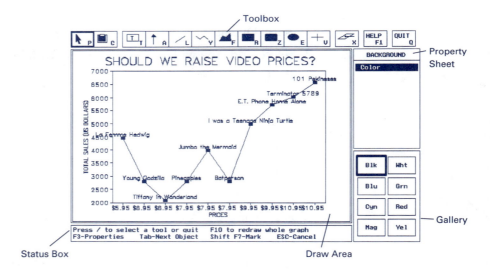

Take a few minutes to examine the screen. The TOTAL SALES graph is displayed in a section called the **draw area**, surrounded by the following sections:

- **Toolbox** (top row) contains pictures, called **icons**, each of which represents a particular feature of the annotator. You can use the icons to create parts of your graph, called **elements**, to enter Edit mode or to exit the annotator. It is the annotator equivalent of the menu bar on the spreadsheet screen. To activate it, type [/].

- **Property Sheet** (top right box) lists adjustable properties of the chosen elements. When you first enter the annotator, the element listed is the background. If you have a color monitor, it can be adjusted by changing the color.

Lesson 8/ Annotating Graphs   99

- **Gallery** (bottom right box) lists available options for the Property Sheet. When you first enter the annotator, it lists possible colors for the background.
- **Status Box** (below Draw Area) displays messages to guide you through the annotator.

CREATING A TEXT BOX

To create a text box, choose Text Box from the Toolbox by typing / and then **T**. Move to where you wish the text box to go, type a period, enter the text, and press [Enter]. Follow these steps to create the first text box. Refer to Figure 8-5 to see where to position the boxes.

Figure 8-5
Text boxes

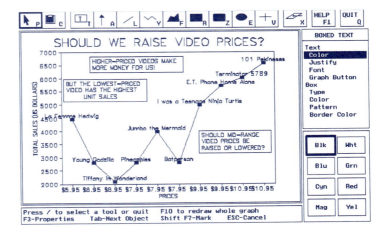

1. Type / to activate the Toolbox.
2. Type **T** to select Text box.

The properties of boxed text appear in the Properties box, and a cursor appears in the middle of the graph.

Use the arrow keys to position the cursor at the top of the graph, just under the **L** in SHOULD in the title. This will be the left edge of the text box.

When the cursor is positioned correctly, type a period to anchor the left edge of the Text box.

If your text will fit all on one line, simply type it in as you normally would. In this case, though, you will want to split the text into two lines. To split text, you must press [Ctrl]-[Enter] (while holding down [Ctrl] press [Enter]) at the end of the first line.

100   First Look at Quattro Pro 2.0/3.0

1. Type **HIGHER-PRICED VIDEOS MAKE** and press Ctrl-Enter

2. Type **MORE MONEY FOR US!** and press Enter

The first text box is complete. Notice that Quattro Pro assumes that you still want to use the Text box tool, so it is still activated. Also notice that Quattro Pro has only redrawn part of the graph, to save time. To see the complete graph, press F10.

For the second text box, move the cursor to just inside the left edge of the graph, by the 6000. (Refer to Figure 8-5.) Type a period to anchor it. Then,

1. Type **BUT THE LOWEST-PRICED** and press Ctrl-Enter

2. Type **VIDEO HAS THE HIGHEST** amd press Ctrl-Enter

3. Type **UNIT SALES**.

Use the spacebar when typing the beginning of the third line to position UNIT SALES in the center of the line. When done,

1. Press Enter

2. Press F10 to see the complete graph.

For the final text box, move the cursor to the lower right corner of the graph and the 4000 level. (Refer to Figure 8-5.) Type a period to anchor it.

1. Type **SHOULD MID-RANGE** and press Ctrl-Enter

2. Type **VIDEO PRICES BE,** and press Ctrl-Enter

3. Type **RAISED OR LOWERED?** and press Enter

This completes the third text box.

Press F10 to view the completed text boxes (Figure 8-5).

■ ■ ■ ■ ■ ■ ■ ■ ■
DRAWING ARROWS

The next step is to draw arrows pointing to the video names.

1. Type / to activate the Toolbox.

2. Type **A** to select the Arrow from the Toolbox.

The Properties box now displays Arrow properties, and the cursor is, once again, in the center of the graph.

For the first graph, use the arrow keys to position the cursor on the right side of the box (refer to Figure 8-6). This will be the base of the arrow.

1. Type a period to anchor the arrow.

Lesson 8/ Annotating Graphs   **101**

Figure 8-6
Arrows

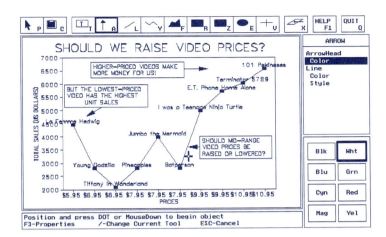

2. Press → to extend the arrow until the cursor is under the **O** in VIDEO.

3. Press Enter

The arrowhead appears, and the arrow is completed.

For the second arrow, position the cursor at the bottom center of the second box, under the **S** in SALES (refer to Figure 8-6).

1. Type a period to anchor the arrow.

2. Use the arrow keys to extend the arrow diagonally so that it is pointing at La Femme Hedwig.

3. Press Enter

Again, the arrowhead appears.

For the final arrow, position the cursor on the left side of the third box.

1. Type a period to anchor the arror, and use the arrow keys to extend it until it is pointing at the midrange videos.

2. Press Enter to complete the arrow.

You have completed the graph annotation (Figure 8-6).

QUITTING THE ANNOTATOR

To leave the Graph Annotator,

1. Press / to activate the Toolbox.

2. Type **Q** to Quit.

102   First Look at Quattro Pro 2.0/3.0

You are returned to the main /Graph menu.

Press F10 to display the graph. The graph data and annotations are clearly displayed. Design purists, though, might consider the graph a little too cluttered. As you become more experienced with Quattro Pro's Graph and Annotator features, you will be better able to judge what kind of graphs present your data most effectively.

For now, press Esc to return to the main /Graph menu.

SAVING CHANGES TO A GRAPH

To save changes to a graph, you must select /Graph│Name│Create again. If you use the /Graph│Customize Series│Reset│Graph command to reset all settings, you will lose all your changes. When the changes involve annotation, it can be especially tedious to redo them!

NOTE: If you have Quattro PRO 3.0 and Autosave Edits is set to **On***, the changes will be saved automatically when you start working on a new graph.*

To save changes, from the main /Graph menu:

1. Select **Name│Create**.

   The graph name window appears.

2. Place the highlight on TOTAL SALES if it is not there already, and press Enter.

   The new annotations are now saved.

Now that you have saved the changed graph, reset the graph settings.

1. Select **Customize Series│Reset│Graph**.

2. Press Esc twice to return to the spreadsheet.

Save the spreadsheet. Be sure to specify Replace. When you are done, exit Quattro Pro.

■ SUMMARY OF COMMANDS

Topic or Feature	Command or Reference	Menu	Page
Annotate a Graph	Annotator	/Graph│ Annotate	98

Lesson 8/ Annotating Graphs **103**

Topic or Feature	Command or Reference	Menu	Page
Draw an Arrow	Annotator	/Graph ⁞ Annotate,/,A	100
Draw a Text Box	Annotator	/Graph ⁞ Annotate, /,T	99
Exit the Annotator	Annotator	/Graph ⁞ Annotate,/,Q	101
Remove Grid Lines	Grid Lines	/Graph ⁞ Overall ⁞ Grid ⁞ Clear	97
Reset Graph Settings	Graph Reset	/Graph ⁞ Customize Series ⁞ Reset ⁞ Graph	94
Retrieve a Spreadsheet	Retrieve	/File ⁞ Retrieve	94
Save a Modified Graph	Graph Name	/Graph ⁞ Name ⁞ Create	102

SELF-TEST

1. Why would you annotate a graph? _____
   _____.

2. What is the difference between /File ⁞ **Open** and /File ⁞ **Retrieve**? _____
   _____
   _____.

3. When you reset graph settings, will you lose named graphs? _____.

4. When you reset graph settings, will you lose the current graph if you have
   not saved it with a name? _____.

5. On what menu will you find options concerning grid lines? _____
   _____.

6. In the annotator, the part of the screen where the graph is displayed is
   called the _____ .

7. The top row of the annotator contains the _____ .

8. List two items you can choose from the Toolbox. _____
   _____.

104 First Look at Quattro Pro 2.0/3.0

9. Where is the status box of the annotator located? What does it do?

_____

_____.

10. Press _____ to start a new line in a text box.

11. Press _____ to quit the annotator.

LESSON NINE: Linking Spreadsheets

OBJECTIVES

At the end of this lesson, you will be able to:

- Open more than one spreadsheet at a time.
- Display spreadsheets in more than one window.
- Move within windows.
- Zoom in and out of a window.
- Move between windows.
- Create formulas that link two spreadsheets.
- Change linked references.
- Create functions that link two spreadsheets.
- Use the @IF function with linked spreadsheets.
- Hide spreadsheet columns.

So far, you have been working with one spreadsheet at a time. But there might be reasons for working with more than one. Suppose, for instance, that you are a highly paid computer consultant and the spreadsheet you developed in Lessons Two through Four were the travel expenses incurred while working for one client. You have many more clients, each requiring separate spreadsheets. How can you keep track of your total travel expenses? Or suppose that you want to buy a yacht and an airplane as well as a classic car. The information on monthly payments for each purchase is on a separate spreadsheet. How can you find out what your total monthly payments will be? Or suppose that instead of managing just one video store you manage five of them and keep the inventory for each on a separate spreadsheet. How can you combine the information to make intelligent marketing decisions?

You could put all the information into one huge spreadsheet. But you can see only one screen at a time, and you may lose track of the cells which you used to store some vital information. Besides, printing out such a huge spreadsheet is very awkward, even with the printing techniques you will learn in Lesson Ten. For those reasons, Quattro Pro lets you link spreadsheets. You learned in Lesson Five how to link cells in one part of a spreadsheet to cells in another part by using cell addresses. To link to cells in a different spreadsheet, you include the name of that spreadsheet in the cell address. For example, if you are at cell K24 in spreadsheet TOTAL.WQ1 and want to link to cell B4 in the same spreadsheet, type **+B4**. Similarly, if you are at cell K24 in spreadsheet TOTAL.WQ1 and want to link to cell B4 in the spreadsheet EXPENSES.WQ1, enter the cell reference **+[EXPENSES]B4** in a formula. The brackets, [ ], are part of the cell reference and must be included. A cell reference that refers (points) to a cell in another spreadsheet is a **link** to that spreadsheet. The link behaves like any other spreadsheet cell reference: If B4 in EXPENSES is changed, K24 in TOTAL is updated accordingly. You can use a link in any formula, function, or block where you would ordinarily specify a cell address. If the suffix of the spreadsheet file is WQ1, the default, you do not need to include it in the link. If the linked spreadsheet is in the same disk drive and directory as the main spreadsheet, you do not need to include the disk drive and directory in the link either. Just use the filename of the spreadsheet. If the linked spreadsheet is in a different directory or disk drive, you do need to specify the directory or spreadsheet in the link.

A link works even if the linked spreadsheet is not Open, but it can be easier to create the link if you see the two spreadsheets side by side. In this lesson, you will create a spreadsheet with links to the three spreadsheets you have already created. You will also learn how to split the screen into different **windows** to make it easier to work with two spreadsheets at once. Finally, you will learn new ways of controlling which rows and columns Quattro Pro displays on the screen.

Begin by creating a new spreadsheet. If you have just started Quattro Pro, SHEET1.WQ1 should be displayed.

1. Move to D1.

2. Type **LINKING SPREADSHEETS** and press ⌷Enter⌷

Next, use ⌷Ctrl⌷-⌷S⌷ to save the spreadsheet as LINK.WQ1, which will make it easier for you to determine which spreadsheet you are working on.

The first spreadsheet you will link to is EXPENSES.WQ1. To clarify this, add the following labels in LINK to cells A3 through A10:

	A
3	**ITEMIZED TRAVEL EXPENSES**
4	
5	**Seattle:**
6	**New York:**
7	**Montreal:**
8	**Paris:**
9	
10	**TOTAL EXPENSES:**

You are now ready to open EXPENSES.WQ1.

OPENING AND DISPLAYING MORE THAN ONE SPREADSHEET

You can use /File|Open to open as many as 32 different spreadsheets at a time. When you first open a new spreadsheet, Quattro Pro displays it on top of the already-open spreadsheet, as though you just placed a new sheet of paper on top of the old one. To display all open spreadsheets next to each other on the screen, as though they were two pieces of paper placed side by side, activate the /Windows menu and select Tile. This feature is called "Tile" because the spreadsheets are displayed as if they were little tiles placed flat on the screen. The shortcut key for the /Windows|Tile command is Ctrl-T.

To open EXPENSES and display it next to LINK:

1. Select /File|Open, and choose EXPENSES.WQ1.

   EXPENSES will be displayed on the screen on top of LINK. It will take up the full screen, as it would if no other spreadsheet were open. The only indication you have that another spreadsheet is already open is that at the bottom left corner of the screen, just to the right of EXPENSES.WQ1, you will see [2].

2. Press Ctrl-T (or /Window|Tile)

   This displays both spreadsheets, side by side. EXPENSES.WQ1 should be on the left and LINK.WQ1 on the right (Figure 9-1).

Figure 9-1
Displaying spreadsheets side by side (tiled)

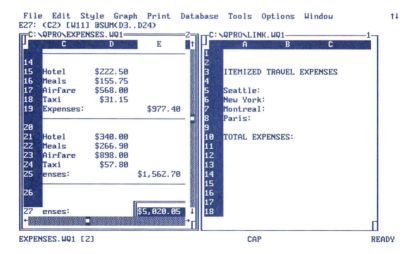

At this point, the screen is divided into two different **windows**, with a separate spreadsheet in each window. The name of the spreadsheet is at the top

108   First Look at Quattro Pro 2.0/3.0

left of the window, and the window number is at the top right (refer to Figure 9-1). LINK.WQ1 is currently in window 1, and EXPENSES.WQ1 is currently in window 2.

Moving Within Windows

To display both spreadsheets at once, Quattro Pro has split the screen in half, which means it can display only half a spreadsheet's usual width. The rest of the spreadsheet is still there, though, and you can use all the usual keys to move around it. You should still be in EXPENSES.WQ1. Practice moving around the spreadsheet:

1. Press [Home] to move to A1 if you are not there already.

2. Press [F5], type **C33**, and press [Enter] to move to C33.

3. Press [→] 10 times to move to M33.

4. Press [Home] to return to A1.

The command menu will also work as usual for the spreadsheet the highlight is in. It will ignore the other spreadsheet. To demonstrate this feature, try inserting a column at A1 in EXPENSES:

1. Press [Ctrl]-[I]

2. Select **C**olumn.

3. Press [Enter] to insert a column at A1.

As you can see, it worked just as you would expect. Now delete the column:

1. Select /**E**dit ⌐**D**elete.

2. Select **C**olumn.

3. Press [Enter]

The column is deleted.

Zooming In to a Window

If you find working with half the usual spreadsheet too constraining, use the /**W**indow ⌐**Z**oom command to expand the spreadsheet to its regular size. The shortcut key for this is [Alt]-[F6] (while holding down [Alt], press [F6]). This allows you to zoom in to a particular spreadsheet, as if you had a zoom lens on a camera. When you want the "wide-angle" view again to see both spreadsheets at once, press [Alt]-[F6] again.

To zoom in to EXPENSES.WQ1,

1. Press [Alt]-[F6] (or /**W**indow ⌐**Z**oom)

Lesson 9/ Linking Spreadsheets   **109**

The spreadsheet is displayed at its usual width. To zoom back out,

2. Press [Alt]-[F6]

Both spreadsheets are again displayed side by side.

Moving Between Windows

You cannot move between windows by pressing [→] or [←]. Instead, you can use the /**W**indow ⏐**Pick** command. This command is especially useful if you have many spreadsheets open. /**W**indow ⏐**Pick** will display a list of open spreadsheets; to pick one, type its number, or use the arrow keys to highlight it and press [Enter]. Try using /**W**indow ⏐**Pick** to move to LINK.

1. Select /**W**indow ⏐**Pick**.

   A window appears with the names of the two open files.

2. Move the highlight to LINK and press [Enter]

   The highlight appears in LINK at the cell where you last left it.

If you only have a few spreadsheets open, a quicker way to move from one to the other is to press [Alt] and the number of the window you want to move to. That is, if you want to move to window 1, press [Alt]-[1] (while holding down [Alt], press [1]). To move to window 2, press [Alt]-[2], and so on. Practice using this technique to move back and forth between LINK and EXPENSES.

1. Press [Alt]-[2] to move to EXPENSES.

2. Press [Alt]-[1] to move back to LINK.

CREATING LINKS IN FORMULAS

Now that you have practice moving within and between windows, you are ready to create links. In this case, you will create cell references in LINK to display the expenses for each trip in EXPENSES. Then you will total them in LINK and see how changes in EXPENSES affect LINK.

1. Press [Alt]-[2] to move to EXPENSES.

2. Use [→] to arrange the spreadsheet on the screen to that trip expenses, columns C through E, are displayed. To start, make sure that rows 1–18 are displayed as well (refer to Figure 9-2).

3. Press [Alt]-[1] to return to LINK.

Figure 9-2
Linked cell reference

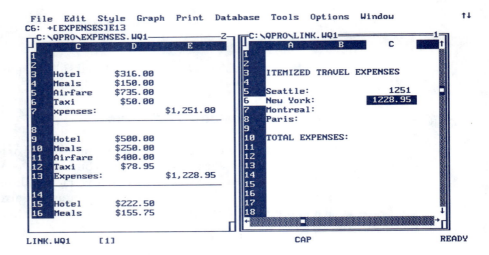

4. Move to C5.

To display the expenses for Seattle, in EXPENSES, E7,

1. Type **+[EXPENSES]E7** and press [Enter]

C5 in LINK should display 1251. The + lets Quattro Pro know you are typing a formula. Otherwise, the cell reference would be displayed as a label.

To display the expenses for New York,

1. Move to C6.

2. Type **+[EXPENSES]E13** and press [Enter]

C6 in LINK should display 1228.95 (Figure 9-2).

To make it easier to create links to the remaining cities' expenses, change the rows in EXPENSES displayed on the screen.

1. Press [Alt]-[2] to return to EXPENSES.

2. Press [Pg Dn] to display rows 19–38 (refer to Figure 9-3).

3. Press [Alt]-[1] to return to LINK.

4. Move to C7.

To display expenses for Montreal, type **+[EXPENSES]E19** and press [Enter]

C7 in LINK should display 977.4.

To display the expenses for Paris,

1. Move to C8.

2. Type **+[EXPENSES]E25** and press [Enter]

Figure 9-3
@SUM with linked references

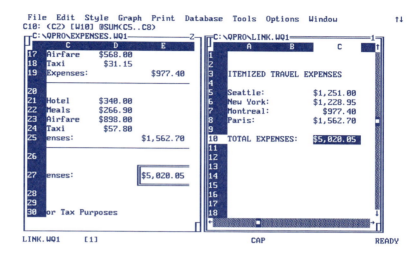

C8 in LINK should display 1562.7.

These linked references can be used in formulas. To demonstrate, move to C10 in LINK and enter the formula @SUM(C5..C8):

1. Move to C10.

2. Type **@SUM(C5..C8)** and press Enter

C10 in LINK should display the total, 5020.05. Use Ctrl-W to increase the column width to 10 and Ctrl-F to format cells C5 through C10 in currency format (Figure 9-3).

CHANGING LINKED REFERENCES

Changing any of the linked values in EXPENSES will change the TOTAL EXPENSES value in C10 in LINK. To illustrate, assume that you realize you made a mistake in the Paris airfare, which should be $950, not $898.

1. Press Alt-2 to move to EXPENSES.

2. Move to D23.

3. Type **950** and press Enter

This changes the subtotal for Paris expenses in EXPENSES, E25 to $1,614.70, and it changes the linked value in LINK, C8 to the same amount. The TOTAL EXPENSES values in EXPENSES, E27 and LINK, C10 are changed as well, to $5,072.05.

112   First Look at Quattro Pro 2.0/3.0

Creating Links in Functions

As you can see, using links in formulas is very easy. It is also easy to use them in functions. To illustrate, you will create links between LINK and VIDEO.WQ1. First, close EXPENSES.

1. Press [Alt]-[2] to move to EXPENSES if you are not there already.

2. Press [Ctrl]-[S], and select **R**eplace to save the spreadsheet.

3. Select /**File**|**Close**.

   Quattro Pro closes the window and moves the highlight back to window 1. To expand it to full size,

4. Press [Alt]-[F6] (or /**W**indow|**Z**oom).

@IF FUNCTION

This time, you want to use the data in VIDEO to work out a system for discounting certain video prices. If the total sales for a video are less than $3,000, you want to try a radical solution, discounting the price to $5.95. If the total sales are $3,000 or more, you plan to leave the price as it is. You can use the @IF function, which you learned in Lesson Five, to do this. In this case, the condition is TOTAL SALES<3000, the first value is 5.95, and the second value is the current video price. Start by setting up the labels for the spreadsheet links:

1. Move to E3.

2. Type **VIDEO DISCOUNTS** and press [Enter]

Next, set up the columns. You want to link to the video name in E and the total sales in F. You have to adjust the widths.

3. Press [Ctrl]-[W] to change the width of E to 30 and that of F to 10.

4. Enter the following labels:

	E	F
5	**VIDEO NAME:**	**NEW PRICE:**

5. Finally, move to E7.

Now you are ready to open and display VIDEO.WQ1.

1. Select /**File**|**O**pen, and choose VIDEO.WQ1.

2. Press [Ctrl]-[T] to display it next to LINK.

3. Move to B4 to display video names.

   The two spreadsheets are displayed side by side (Figure 9-4).

Figure 9-4
Linking to
VIDEO.WQ1

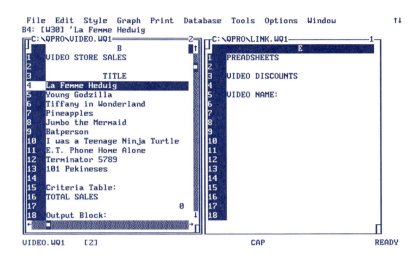

The first link you will create is the video name.

1. Press Alt-1 to move to LINK.

2. Move to E7 if you are not there already.

3. Type **+[VIDEO]B4** and press Enter

This creates a link to the first video title, La Femme Hedwig. La Femme Hedwig is displayed in LINK, E7.

Next, enter the function, but before doing that you should adjust the way VIDEO is displayed. Press Alt-2 to move to VIDEO, and press → to display PRICE.

Look at the window. You want to display PRICE and TOTAL SALES since those are the two columns you will refer to in the @IF function. Unfortunately, the window is too small. UNIT SALES is between PRICE and TOTAL SALES; therefore, you can display either PRICE and UNIT SALES or UNIT SALES and TOTAL SALES, but not PRICE and TOTAL SALES. If only there were some way to temporarily remove UNIT SALES from view! Fortunately, there is: the **H**ide Column feature on the **/S**tyle menu.

HIDING COLUMNS

To hide a column, first position the highlight on the column you want to hide. Then select /**S**tyle ǀ **H**ide Column ǀ **H**ide. To display the column again, select /**S**tyle ǀ **H**ide Column ǀ **E**xpose. To hide the UNIT SALES column,

1. Position the highlight at D4 (you could place it anywhere in column D).

114   First Look at Quattro Pro 2.0/3.0

2. Select /Style ¦Hide Column.

3. Select **Hide**. The input line will read: "Hide column from view: D4".

4. Press [Enter]

Column D is hidden, and the PRICE and TOTAL SALES columns are displayed side by side. Notice that column D has not been erased; the column letters just skip from C to E.

Now you are ready to enter the formula in LINK.

1. Press [Alt]-[1] to move to LINK.

2. Press [→] to move to F7.

3. Type **@IF([VIDEO]E4<3000,5.95,[VIDEO]C4)**

   This function tells Quattro Pro to look at cell E4 in VIDEO. If the value is less than 3,000, the value 5.95 should be displayed. If cell E4 is 3,000 or more, the value in cell C4 in VIDEO, the current price, should be displayed. When typing, be sure to include all parentheses and brackets.

4. Press [Enter]

   5.95 is displayed in LINK, F7. If you look at VIDEO, C4 and E4, you can see why. Total sales for La Femme Hedwig are greater than $3,000, so the price, $5.95, stays the same.

5. Press [Ctrl]-[F] to format LINK, F7 for currency.

To apply the same formula to the rest of the videos, all you have to do is copy LINK, E7 and F7 to block E8..F16. Since the links use relative cell addresses and are arranged in a list, the copies will automatically link to the proper cells. To copy the cells,

1. Press [Alt]-[F6] to display LINK full size.

2. Move to E7.

3. Press [Shift]-[F7], and extend the block through F7.

4. Press [Ctrl]-[C]

5. Move the highlight to E8 and type a period. Extend the block through E16.

6. Press [Enter]

   Quattro Pro displays the videos with their new prices. To check to see if the calculation worked, display the two spreadsheets side by side again:

7. Press [Alt]-[F6] to zoom out.

8. Press [↓] to adjust LINK so that the prices are even with the prices in VIDEO (Figure 9-5).

As you can see, in each case where TOTAL SALES in VIDEO are below

Lesson 9/ Linking Spreadsheets   **115**

Figure 9-5
@IF with linked cell references

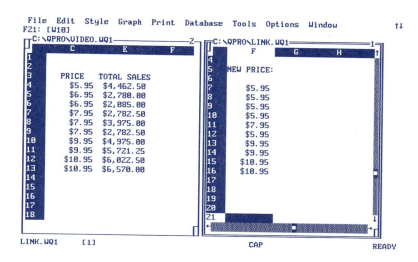

$3,000, the NEW PRICE in LINK is listed as $5.95. You can test the links by changing TOTAL SALES value in VIDEO and watching the effect in LINK.

1. Press Ctrl-S to save LINK, and specify **R**eplace. Then, move to VIDEO and expose the hidden column D.

2. Press Alt-2 to move to VIDEO.

3. Select /**S**tyle ǀ **H**ide Column ǀ **E**xpose.

4. Move the highlight to column D, and press Enter.

5. Press Ctrl-S and specify **R**eplace to save VIDEO. Then exit Quattro Pro.

■ SUMMARY OF COMMANDS

Topic or Feature	Command or Reference	Menu	Page
Display All Open Spreadsheets Side by Side	Ctrl-T	/Windows ǀ Tile	107
Expose a Hidden Column	Hide Columns	/Style ǀ Hide Column ǀ Expose	113
Hide a Column	Hide Columns	/Style ǀ Hide Column ǀ Hide	113
Link Cell Reference	[Filename]Cell Address		110
Move Between Windows	Alt-Window Number	/Window ǀ Pick	109

Topic or Feature	Command or Reference	Menu	Page
Open More Than One Spreadsheet	Open	/File !Open	107
Zoom In to a Window	`Alt`-`F6`	/Window !Zoom	108
Zoom Out from a Window	`Alt`-`F6`	/Window !Zoom	109

■ *SELF-TEST*

1. You are at cell B1 of ONE.WQ1, and you want to create a link to cell C19 of TWO.WQ1. What must you type? _____
   _____.

2. When you open two spreadsheets at once, how are they initially displayed? _____
   _____.

3. To display two open spreadsheets side by side, press _____.

4. If an open spreadsheet takes up only half the screen and you want to zoom in to it, press _____.

5. To zoom back out again, press _____.

6. What are the two ways to move between windows? _____
   _____.

7. Can you tell by looking at a spreadsheet whether or not a column is hidden? If so, how? _____
   _____.

Printing Spreadsheets and Graphs

OBJECTIVES

At the end of this lesson, you will be able to:

- Include report-quality features when printing spreadsheets.
- Insert page breaks.
- Set headers and footers.
- Include page number and date on your spreadsheet.
- Preview your work before printing it.
- Adjust the printer.
- Interrupt printing.
- Divide wide spreadsheets into pages by setting margins.
- Retrieve or open a spreadsheet with links.
- Create headers from row and column labels.
- Print graphs in landscape or portrait orientation.

You already know how to print a block of a spreadsheet. This lesson will demonstrate how to print the spreadsheet using report features such as headers and footers, page numbers, and page breaks. It will also demonstrate printing graphs. Most of the features you will use are on the /**P**rint menu. You will print the EXPENSES, LINK, and CLASSIC spreadsheets as reports, and you will also print the CLASSIC graph.

Start by using /**F**ile|**O**pen to open EXPENSES. If you have not opened it since closing it in the last lesson, it will appear in a half-size window. To have it displayed in full size, press [Alt]-[F6]

INSERTING PAGE BREAKS

The first step in setting up the spreadsheet for printing is to separate the two sections of the spreadsheet into two separate pages. If you do not do this, Quattro Pro will insert its own page breaks, which may come in the middle of a block of data you would prefer to keep together. To set page breaks, use the

118 First Look at Quattro Pro 2.0/3.0

command /**St**yle|**I**nsert Break. Move to the first column in the row in which you wish to set the page breaks. It should be the row *above* where you wish the new page to start. In this case, that row is row 29.

1. Move to A29.
2. Select /**St**yle|**I**nsert Break.

Quattro Pro inserts two colons (::) and an additional line to indicate that a page break has been set.

NOTE: You could also have typed the two colons yourself. Quattro Pro would have interpreted that as a page break during printing.

SETTING HEADERS AND FOOTERS

To set headers and footers, use the Layout feature on the main /**Print** menu.

1. Select /**P**rint|**L**ayout.

    The /**P**rint|**L**ayout menu appears (Figure 10-1).

Figure 10-1
Layout menu

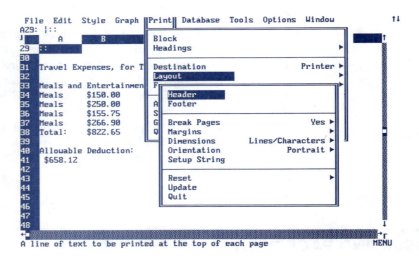

2. Select **H**eader.

    A window appears, with the prompt: "A line of text to be printed at the top of each page:".

Lesson 10/ Printing Spreadsheets and Graphs **119**

3. Type **TRAVEL EXPENSES FOR BUSINESS TRIPS** and press Enter

This enters the text as the header. The procedure for specifying a footer is similar. For the footer, though, you want Quattro Pro to print the page number and date. For that, you must use special symbols.

When you type:	Quattro Pro will:
#	Print the page number
@	Print the date
No vertical bar	Left-align the text you enter
¦	Center the text you enter
¦¦	Right-align the text you enter

In the header you just entered, for example, Quattro Pro will left-align the text because you did not include a vertical bar. For the footer, you would like to have the date left-aligned and the page number right-aligned, so, from the **Layout** menu,

1. Select **Footer**.

2. Type @ ¦¦**page #** and press Enter

Here, @ tells Quattro Pro to print the date, left-aligned and ¦¦page # tells Quattro Pro to print the word "page" followed by the page number, right-aligned.

Your last task before printing is to select the block to print.

1. Select **Quit** to return to the main **/Print** menu.

2. Select **B**lock.

3. Move to A1, type a period, extend the block through G47, and press Enter

. . . .
USING SCREEN PREVIEW

At this point you could print the block. But generally it is a good idea to use Quattro Pro's **S**creen Preview feature, found on the **/Print** ¦**Destination** menu. This feature lets you see what your spreadsheet or graph will look like before printing. That way, if you don't like the way it looks, you can change headers, footers, or other features. You choose **S**creen Preview from the **D**estination menu, as though you were printing a kind of printer. Once you have chosen it, select **S**preadsheet Print, as you would if you were going to print it. Instead of sending the spreadsheet or graph to a printer, though, Quattro Pro sends it to the screen. From the main **/Print** menu,

1. Select **D**estination.
2. Select **S**creen Preview.

   The words "Screen Preview" appear next to Destination on the **/P**rint menu.

3. Select **S**preadsheet Print to preview the spreadsheet.

   The Screen Preview screen will appear, displaying the first page of the spreadsheet report. To zoom in to see it better,

4. Type +

   This displays the top part of the page, showing the header (refer to Figure 10-2). The upper right corner of the screen contains a miniature of the entire page, with a **zoom box** showing the position of the section currently displayed. To see the bottom half of the page with the footer,

Figure 10-2
Screen preview, top half of page

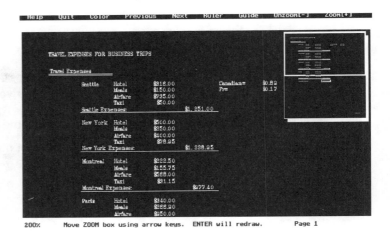

5. Press [↓] repeatedly.

   The box on the miniature page will move down. When it covers the bottom half of the spreadsheet, press [Enter]. The bottom half of the spreadsheet will be displayed (Figure 10-3).

   To see the second page of the spreadsheet,

   1. press [Pg Dn]. This time, you will first be shown the bottom half of the spreadsheet since the zoom box is still positioned on it. Notice that the footer now reads "page 2."

   2. Press [↑] to position the zoom box so that it covers the top half of the page.

   3. Press [Enter]

Figure 10-3
Screen preview,
bottom half of page

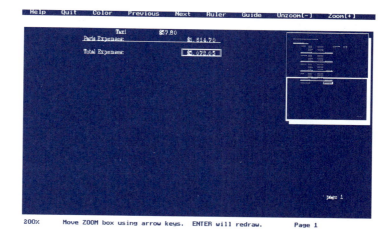

The header, as you can see, has been printed across the top of this page as well. Take time to practice using + to zoom in to the report, – to zoom out, ↑ and ↓ to move the zoom box, and Pg Up and Pg Dn to move back and forth between pages.

PRINTING A SPREADSHEET REPORT

Screen Preview showed that the spreadsheet was indeed set up correctly. You can now print it.

1. Press Esc to leave Spreadsheet Preview and return to the main /**P**rint menu.
2. Select **D**estination.
3. Select **G**raphics Printer.

NOTE: If your spreadsheet report includes presentation-quality features such as drawn lines, you must specify Graphics Printer, rather than the default printer.

Make sure the printer is turned on and ready to print. Use **A**djust Printer **!** **A**lign to make sure Quattro Pro is set up to begin printing at the top of the page.

1. Select **A**djust Printer. The choices are:

   Skip Line

   Form Feed

   Align

122 First Look at Quattro Pro 2.0/3.0

2. Select **A**lign.

3. Finally, to print, select **S**preadsheet Print.

In a few minutes, you will have the printed spreadsheet report. Depending on your printer, you may have to select **/P**rint ¦ **A**djust Printer ¦ **F**orm Feed to print the footer on the second page.

Interrupting Printing

If you want to interrupt printing for some reason, press Ctrl - Break (while holding down Ctrl , press Break).

Saving Print Settings

To save print settings, just save the spreadsheet. The settings are saved automatically. From the main **/P**rint menu,

1. Select **Q**uit.

2. Press Ctrl - S , and specify **R**eplace.

DIVIDING WIDE SPREADSHEETS INTO PAGES

In the last example, you divided your EXPENSES report into pages using **S**tyle ¦ **I**nsert Break because it was too long to fit on a single page. The page break told Quattro Pro to place the first 29 rows on page 1 and the next 20 rows on page 2. But what happens if the spreadsheet is too wide to fit on a single page and you want to divide it up by columns? Quattro Pro does not provide a single page-break command for columns, but it does allow you to set margins for your report, and you can set them so that only a certain number of columns will fit on the page. Quattro Pro will place the remaining columns on the next page. The next section illustrates this process using LINK.

RETRIEVING A LINKED SPREADSHEET

When you use **/F**ile ¦ **R**etrieve or **/F**ile ¦ **O**pen to display a spreadsheet with links, Quattro Pro presents you with several options for dealing with those links.

Lesson 10/ Printing Spreadsheets and Graphs **123**

1. Select /**File**｜**Retrieve**, and specify LINK.WQ1.

A window appears with the following Link Options:

Load Supporting

Update Refs

None

If you want to display the supporting spreadsheets along with LINK, choose **Load Supporting**. **U**pdate Refs maintains the links but does not open the other spreadsheet. **N**one does not maintain the links; the cells with linked references will change to read "NA" (not available). In this case, you want to maintain the links but not display the supporting spreadsheets.

2. Select **U**pdate Refs.
3. Press ⌈Alt⌉-⌈F6⌉ to display the spreadsheet full size.
4. Press ⌈Home⌉ to move to A1.

. . . .
SETTING MARGINS

In LINK, columns A through D link to EXPENSES, whereas columns E through F link to VIDEO. Therefore, it makes sense to print the first four columns on one page and the rest on the next page. That means that the report should be 40 characters wide, since each of the four columns is 9 characters wide with one character as a separator. The command for setting margins is /**Print**｜**Layout**｜**Margins**.

1. Select /**Print**｜**Layout**｜**Margins**.
2. Select **Left**; at the prompt, type **20** and press ⌈Enter⌉
3. Select **Right**; at the prompt, type **60** and press ⌈Enter⌉
4. Press ⌈Esc⌉ to return to the /**Print**｜**Layout** menu.

Now, enter a header and footer:

1. Select **Header**.
2. Type **LINKING SPREADSHEET** and press ⌈Enter⌉
3. Select **Footer**.
4. Type ｜**Page #** and press ⌈Enter⌉
5. Press ⌈Esc⌉ to return to the /**Print** menu.

To print,

124   First Look at Quattro Pro 2.0/3.0

1. Select **B**lock, and specify A3..F6.

2. Select **S**preadsheet Print.

The spreadsheet report will be printed on two pages. Press Ctrl-S and specify **R**eplace to save the print settings with the spreadsheet.

For the next examples, you will use the CLASSIC spreadsheet. Use /**File** **R**etrieve to display CLASSIC.WQ1 and close EXPENSES.WQ1.

■ ■ ■ ■ ■ ■ ■ ■ ■ ■
CREATING HEADINGS FROM ROW AND COLUMN LABELS

In this spreadsheet, you have already set up a title, "Classic Cars," as well as column headings. Since the title and column headings will make a perfectly good header for the printed spreadsheet, you don't need to add an additional header. Instead, you can use /**Print** **Headings** and specify the block you want to use as the heading.

1. Select /**Print** **Headings**,

A pop-up menu is displayed, presenting you with two choices, **Left** Heading and **Top** Heading. A **Left** Heading prints at the left side of each page and consists of one or more columns. It is useful when you have many columns to print. For example, if in addition to MAKE, MODEL, YEAR, and PRICE for each car you also had NAME, ADDRESS, and TELEPHONE NUMBER of previous owners, Quattro Pro would not be able to fit all the information on one page. The information on MAKE, MODEL, YEAR, and PRICE would be printed on one page, and NAME, ADDRESS, and TELEPHONE NUMBER would be printed on the next. To figure out which owner went with each car, you would have to paste the two pages together. If you specified the columns with the car make and model as the left headings, though, that information would be printed on all pages of the report.

A **Top** Heading prints at the top of the page and consists of one or more rows. It works the same way as left headings, only using rows instead of columns. If there are too many rows to print on a single page, the top heading will be printed above the column on the rest of the pages as well. Since that is the case in this example,

1. Select **T**op Heading.

   The input line reads: "Column headings to print across the top of each page:".

2. Move to A1, type a period , extend the block to G4, and press Enter

You are returned to the main /**Print** menu, where the heading block is now defined.

Lesson 10/ Printing Spreadsheets and Graphs **125**

This spreadsheet will fit on one page, so you don't need page breaks or page numbers in the footer. It is often a good idea, though, to include the date in a spreadsheet report to help you keep track of your work. You will therefore create a footer with today's date.

Create the footer:

1. Select **L**ayout.

2. Select **F**ooter.

3. Type @ and press (Enter)

4. Select **Q**uit.

Next, specify the block to be printed. In this case, since you specified A1 through G4 as the heading block, do not specify it for the printing block, or the title and column labels will be printed twice. Instead, specify A5 through H34. Select **B**lock, and specify A5..H34.

If you want to preview the spreadsheet report, select **D**estination ¦**S**creen Preview, and then **S**preadsheet Print. The report will be displayed on the screen. When you are ready to print,

1. Select **D**estination ¦**G**raphics Printer.

2. Select **S**preadsheet Print.

The report will be printed. Select **Q**uit to return to the spreadsheet.

. . . .
SETTING UP A GRAPH TO PRINT

For the next example, you will print the graph CLASSIC. Start by displaying it.

1. Select /**G**raph.

2. Select **N**ame ¦**D**isplay, and specify CLASSIC.

    CLASSIC is displayed, exactly as you left it.

3. Press (Esc) twice to return to the spreadsheet.

Graph Layout Settings

You have several options for printing graphs. To see the options, bring up the Layout menu from the /**P**rint ¦**G**raph Print menu (Figure 10-4).

1. Select /**P**rint ¦**G**raph Print ¦**L**ayout.
    This menu lets you specify top, bottom, and side margins for the graph.

Figure 10-4
Graph layout menu

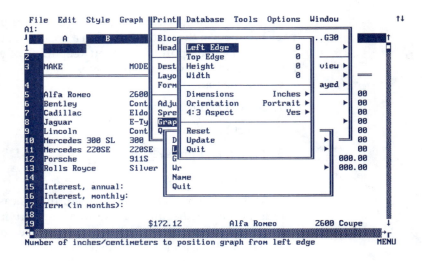

Orientation allows you to print the graph in Portrait form, upright on the page (see Figure 10-5), or Landscape, sideways on the page (see Figure 10-6). For now, leave the settings alone.

Figure 10-5
Graph screen preview, Portrait orientation

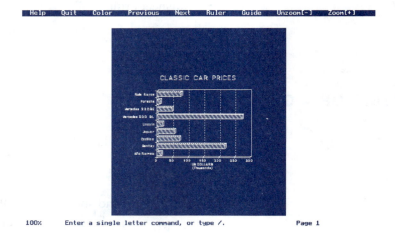

2. Select **Q**uit to return to the **G**raph Print menu.

Previewing a Graph

To preview a graph, from the **G**raph Print menu,

1. Select **D**estination.
2. Select **S**creen Preview.

Figure 10-6
Graph screen preview, Landscape orientation

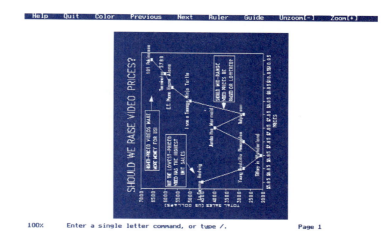

The words "Screen Preview" appear next to **Destination** on the **Graph Print** menu. To preview the graph,

3. Select **G**o.

The graph is displayed on the Screen Preview screen (Figure 10-5).

4. Use + and – to zoom in and out. When done, press Esc

Printing a Graph

To print a graph, from the **Graph Print** menu:

1. Select **D**estination, and specify **G**raph Printer.

   "Graph Printer" is displayed next to **Destination** on the **Graph Print** menu.

2. Select **G**o.

   The graph will be printed. It may take a few minutes. If you wish to interrupt printing, use Ctrl - Break.

3. Press Esc twice to return to the spreadsheet.

Use Ctrl - S and specify **R**eplace to save the spreadsheet with the graph print settings.

As a final exercise, follow these instructions to print TOTAL SALES from VIDEO in Landscape orientation:

1. Select /**F**ile ¦**R**etrieve, and specify VIDEO.WQ1.

2. Press Alt - F6 to display the graph full size.

3. Select /**G**raph.

128   First Look at Quattro Pro 2.0/3.0

4. Select **N**ame ¦**D**isplay, and specify TOTAL SALES.

TOTAL SALES is displayed.

5. Press [Esc] twice to return to the spreadsheet.

To change the graph layout orientation,

1. Select /**P**rint ¦**G**raph Print ¦**L**ayout.

2. Select **O**rientation.

3. Select **L**andscape.

4. Select **Q**uit to return to the **G**raph Print menu.

To preview the graph,

1. Select **D**estination ¦**S**creen Preview.

2. Select **G**o.

The graph is displayed on the screen. It is sideways, so you can tell it will be printed in Landscape orientation (Figure 10-6).

3. Press [Esc] to return to the **G**raph Print menu.

To print the graph,

1. Select **D**estination ¦**G**raph Printer.

2. Select **G**o.

In a few minutes, the graph will be printed. Press [Esc] twice to return to the spreadsheet. Press [Ctrl]-[S] and specify **R**eplace to save the spreadsheet with the print settings. When you are done, exit Quattro Pro.

This concludes the lesson, and the book. I hope you have enjoyed your first look at Quattro Pro. By now, you should be familiar with many of its most important features and be able to use it in your own applications. Now begin to find out for yourself how Quattro Pro can make your work easier.

■SUMMARY OF COMMANDS

Topic or Feature	Command or Reference	Menu	Page
Adjust Printer before Printing	Adjust Printer	/Print ¦ Adjust Printer ¦ Align	121
Center Text	¦		119
Eject Page from Printer	Adjust Printer	/Print ¦ Adjust Printer ¦ Form Feed	121

Lesson 10/ Printing Spreadsheets and Graphs **129**

Topic or Feature	Command or Reference	Menu	Page
Exit Preview Screen	Esc		127
Footers	Print Layout	/Print¦Layout¦ Footer	119
Headers	Print Layout	/Print¦Layout¦ Header	118
Interrupt Printing	Ctrl-Break		121
Left-Align Text	Default		119
Load a Linked Spreadsheet	Link Options		122
Page Breaks	::	/Style¦ Insert Break	118
Preview Spreadsheet	Screen Preview	/Print¦ Destination¦ Screen Preview	119
Preview Graph	Graph Print	/Print¦ Graph Print¦ Destination¦ Screen Preview	126
Print Graph	Print	/Print¦ Graph Print¦Go	127
Print Orientation	Graph Print	/Print¦ Graph Print¦ Orientation	127
Print Page Number	#		119
Print Date	@		119
Right-Align Text	¦¦		119
Set Up Graphics Printer	Graph Print	/Print¦ Graph Print¦ Destination¦ Graphics Printer	125
Set Margins	Print Layout	/Print¦Layout¦ Margins	123
Use Spreadsheet Titles As Headings	Print	/Print¦Headings	124
Zoom In to Preview	+		120
Zoom Out from Preview	–		120

130 First Look at Quattro Pro 2.0/3.0

■ *SELF-TEST*

1. Your spreadsheet extends from A1 through C49. How can you divide it so that it prints on two pages? _____
_____ .

2. Your spreadsheet extends from A1 through K15. How can you divide it so that it prints on two pages? _____
_____ .

3. List three features you used from the /Print Layout menu.
_____
_____ .

4. Explain the difference between /Print Headings and /Print Layout Header. _____
_____ .

5. What commands should you use to view your spreadsheet before printing it? _____
_____ .

6. What commands should you use to view your graph before printing it?
_____
_____ .

7. When viewing your spreadsheet or graph before printing, press _____ to zoom in to a section.

8. When viewing your spreadsheet or graph before printing, press _____ to zoom out from a section.

9. When viewing your spreadsheet or graph before printing, press _____ or _____ to move the zoom box up or down.

10. _____ orientation means a graph will be printed upright on an 8½″ by 11″ sheet of paper.

11. _____ orientation means a graph will be printed sideways on an 8½″ by 11″ sheet of paper.

12. Press _____ to halt printing.

Using a Mouse with Quattro Pro

If you have a mouse, you can use it to choose Quattro Pro commands and define blocks more quickly than by using the keyboard alone. Quattro Pro automatically detects whether or not you have a mouse. If you do, a pointer will appear on the screen, and on the right side of the screen you will see the **mouse palette**. By positioning the pointer on items in the mouse palette and clicking (quickly pressing and releasing the left mouse button), you can duplicate many of the keyboard features. Refer to Figure A-1 when going through the following list (starting from the top):

Figure A-1
Mouse palette

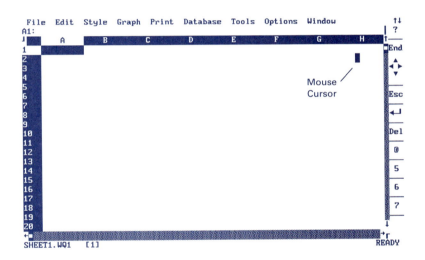

?   Click on this for Help instead of pressing F1.

✧   Click on these arrows instead of pressing End plus arrow keys to move to the end of an area in the given direction.

Esc   Click on this instead of pressing Esc.

⏎   Click on this instead of pressing Enter.

Del   Click on this instead of pressing Del.

@   Click on this instead of pressing Alt - F3 to bring up the Function menu.

131

You can also use a mouse to choose menu commands by simply positioning the pointer on the command and clicking. In any command that presents you with a box with both Enter and Cancel, you can use the mouse to click on the proper choice. Finally, you can use the mouse to point out blocks. To point out a single cell, position the pointer on that cell and click it. To point out a multiple-cell block, first position the pointer on the first cell in that block. Then hold down the mouse button while moving the pointer to the last cell in the block. When the pointer reaches the last cell, release the mouse button. (Moving the pointer while holding down the button this way is called **dragging**.) If the block includes more than one row or column, point it out by dragging the mouse from the cell in one corner diagonally across to the other corner.

You will also find it easier to use a mouse with the Annotating Graph screen. You can select a tool to work with by clicking on it with the mouse. You can also move elements by dragging them with the mouse instead of by using the arrow keys on the keyboard.

Self-Test Answers

LESSON 1

1. Spreadsheet and command menu
2. SHEET1.WQ1
3. by letters, in ascending alphabetical order (A, B, C, …)
4. by numbers, in ascending order (1, 2, 3, …)
5. the intersection of a row and a column, where data are entered
6. The letter comes from the column it is in, and the number comes from the row it is in.
7. Move the highlight up one screen; move it down one screen; move it right one screen; move it left one screen; move it to the cell address specified after pressing `F5`; move it to cell A1.
8. `F2`
9. A label consists of words, but a value consists of numbers or formulas that evaluate to numbers.
10. Position the highlight on the cell and press `Del`.
11. /
12. Type the highlighted letter on the menu bar.
13. Type the highlighted letter for that command or feature, or press the arrow keys until the command or feature is highlighted and press `Enter`.
14. `Esc`
15. `Esc`

LESSON 2

1. Type +, move to B1, type +, move to C3, press `Enter`.
2. relative
3. absolute
4. `F4`
5. @SUM is the function name, B1 is the starting cell, .. is the pointer, B6 is the ending cell. It will add all cell contents from B1 through B6 inclusive.
6. `Alt`-`F3`
7. `Esc`
8. Highlight the cell, press `Ctrl`-`F`, then press C and `Enter`.
9. Cell contents are too wide to be displayed in the current column.
10. Widen the column by pressing `Ctrl`-`W`, specifying the column width in characters, and pressing `Enter`.

LESSON 3

1. **S**ave, **E**xit, **O**pen
2. **I**nsert, **D**elete, **C**opy, **M**ove
3. below
4. to the right
5. Yes; +B8*K20
6. no
7. no
8. **R**eplace
9. Press `Ctrl`-`X` and then select **Y**es.

LESSON 4

1. **N**umeric Format, **C**olumn Width, **L**ine Drawing
2. block
3. You can work with many cells at once, instead of each one individually.
4. `Shift`-`F7`
5. Use `Shift`-`F7` to highlight block E5..G5; then select /**S**tyle |**L**ine Drawing |**B**ottom |**D**ouble.
6. Use `Shift`-`F7` to highlight block E5..G5; then select /**S**tyle |**L**ine Drawing |**B**ottom |**N**one.
7. Delete the row by positioning the highlight on it and selecting /**E**dit |**D**elete |**R**ow.
8. **G**raphics Printer

133

134   Self-Test Answers

9. A1..C15
10. Press [Esc] to remove the message from the screen, then specify a block to print with **/Print ¦Block**.

LESSON 5

1. Use [Shift]-[F7] to highlight the cells; then press [Ctrl]-[A] and select **R**ight.
2. @COUNT
3. @MAX
4. @MIN
5. @PMT
6. amount of principal, interest rate, number of payment periods
7. [F4]
8. +A1
9. **/Tools ¦Solve** For
10. Formula Cell, Target Value, Variable Cell
11. Select **/Tools ¦Solve** For, specify B1 as the Formula cell, 48 as the **T**arget Value, and C1 as the **V**ariable Cell, and select **G**o.
12. @IF
13. Condition; value, label, or formula to use if condition is met; value, label, or formula to use if condition is not met

LESSON 6

1. fields; records
2. field; record
3. when you would like to preserve the original order of your data, so that you can return to it after sorting
4. start value, step value, stop value
5. to let Quattro Pro know the names of database fields
6. Sort key
7. (1) Move the highlight to the column to use as the first sort key and press [Enter]. (2) If you have previously specified **/Database ¦Query ¦Assign** Names, just type the name of the field and press [Enter].
8. criteria table
9. **L**ocate; **E**xtract
10. output block

LESSON 7

1. bar, rotated bar, and line
2. series
3. 6
4. 1
5. [F10]
6. **1**st Line (of graph title), **X**-Title, **Y**-Title
7. **/Graph ¦Customize** Series
8. **/Graph ¦Name ¦Create**, and specify a name
9. You lose the graph.

LESSON 8

1. to clarify what it means, or to emphasize its most important points
2. **/File ¦Open** simply opens a new spreadsheet; **/File ¦Retrieve** closes the currently displayed spreadsheet *and* opens a new one.
3. no
4. yes
5. **/Graph ¦Overall**
6. Draw area
7. Toolbox
8. Text box ([/][T]), Arrow ([/][A])
9. underneath the draw area; displays messages to help you select features of the annotator
10. [Ctrl]-[Enter]
11. [/][Q]

LESSON 9

1. +[TWO]C19[Enter]
2. The most recently opened one is displayed in front of the other.
3. [Ctrl]-[T]
4. [Alt]-[F6]
5. [Alt]-[F6]
6. Select **/Window ¦Pick**, and choose the spreadsheet you wish to work with, or press [Alt] and the number of the window you wish to move to (for example, [Alt]-[2] for window 2).
7. Yes; the column letters will appear to skip a letter.

Self-Test Answers   **135**

LESSON 10

1. Insert a page break using **/Style** **Insert Break** so that half the rows print on one page and half print on the other.
2. Set left and right margins using **/Print** **Layout** **Margins** so that half the columns print on one page and half print on the other.
3. Header, Footer, Margins
4. **/Print** **Headings** allows you to use *existing* row or column labels as top or left headers; **/Print** **Layout** **Header** allows you to specify *new* text to be used as a header.

5. **/Print** **Destination** **Screen Preview**; then **/Print** **Spreadsheet Print**
6. **/Print** **Graph Print** **Destination** **Screen Preview**; then **/Print** **Graph Print** **Go**
7. +
8. –
9. $\boxed{\uparrow}$; $\boxed{\downarrow}$
10. portrait
11. landscape
12. $\boxed{\text{Ctrl}}$–$\boxed{\text{Break}}$

Quattro Pro 2.0/3.0 Command Summary

This Command Summary includes the most frequently used commands in Quattro Pro, including some not discussed in this book. It does not include a list of functions. Commands available only in Quattro Pro version 3.0 are designated (v. 3.0).

Topic or Feature	Command or Reference	Menu	Page
Absolute Cell Addresses	F4		16
Activate Command Menu	/		7
Adding Cells	@SUM		18
Adjust Printer Before Printing	Adjust Printer	/Print ! Adjust Printer ! Align	121
Annotate a Graph	Annotator	/Graph ! Annotate	98
Assign/Delete/Change Names for Blocks	Names	/Edit !Names	
Assign Names to Database Fields	Assign Names	/Database ! Query ! Assign Names	70
Automatically Save Changes to Graphs (v. 3.0)	Autosave Edits	/Graph !Name ! Autosave Edits !On	
Begin a Formula with a Cell Address	+		6
Block	(Beginning cell address .. Ending cell address)		21
Break Long Labels into Cell Entries	Parse	/Tools !Parse	
Cancel an Action	Esc		5
Center Text	!		119
Change Alignment	Ctrl-A	/Style ! Alignment	51
Change Directory	Directory	/File !Directory	
Change Fonts	Font	/Style !Font	
Change Formulas to Values	Values	/Edit !Values	
Change Graph Colors/ Outlines/Grids	Overall	/Graph !Overall	
Clear Locked Titles	Locked Titles	/Window !Options ! Locked Titles ! Clear	

136

Quattro Pro 2.0/ 3.0 Command Summary   **137**

Topic or Feature	Command or Reference	Menu	Page
Close a Spreadsheet	Close	/File |Close	85
Close All Open Files	Close All	/File |Close All	
Close Up Menu	Esc		
Column Width	Ctrl-W	/Style | Column Width	22
Combine Two Blocks or Spreadsheets	Combine	/Tools |Combine	
Comma Format	Ctrl-F, ,	/Style | Numeric Format |,	52
Conditional Statement	@IF		61
Copy a Block of Cells	Mark the block, Ctrl-C	/Edit |Copy	39
Copy a Cell	Ctrl-C	/Edit |Copy	32

Copy a Graph from One
  Spreadsheet to Another
	Graph Copy	/Graph |Name |
		  Graph Copy	

Count	@COUNT		52
Create a Graph	Graph	/Graph	78
Create/Change/Execute/ Delete Macros	Alt-F2	/Tools |Macro	
Currency Format	Ctrl-F, C	/Style | Numeric Format | Currency	21

Data Matrix: Inversion
  or Multiplication
	Invert/Multiply	/Tools |Advanced
		  Math	

Default Color Settings	Color	/Options |Color	

Default Date/Time/
  Currency Settings
	International	/Options |
		  International	

Default Directory/
  File Extension/Menu
  Tree
	Startup	/Options |Startup	

Default Display Mode	Display Mode	/Options |Display Mode	
Default Graphics Quality	Graphics Quality	/Options |Graphics Quality	
Default Hardware Settings	Hardware	/Options |Hardware	

Default Mouse Palette
  Buttons
	Mouse Palette	/Options |Mouse
		  Palette	

Default Undo Settings	Undo	/Options |Other |Undo	
Delete a Block of Cells	Mark the block, Del		7,45
Delete a Column	Delete	/Edit |Delete | Column	31

138 Quattro Pro 2.0/3.0 Command Summary

Topic or Feature	Command or Reference	Menu	Page
Delete a Row	Delete	/Edit !Delete ! Row	30
Delete Data	Del		
Display a Named Graph	Graph Name	/Graph !Name ! Display	84
Display All Open Spreadsheets Side by Side	Ctrl-T	/Windows !Tile	107
Display Graphs At a Set Interval	Slide	/Graph !Name !Slide	
Divide Window into Vertical Panes	Vertical	/Window !Options ! Vertical	
Divide Window into Horizontal Panes	Horizontal	/Window !Options ! Horizontal	
DOS Access	DOS Shell	/File !Utilities ! DOS Shell	
Draw a Text Box	Annotator	/Graph ! Annotate,/,T	99
Draw an Arrow	Annotator	/Graph ! Annotate,/,A	100
Draw Double Lines Below Cells	Line Drawing	/Style ! Line Drawing ! Bottom !Double	
Draw Double-Lined Boxes	Line Drawing	/Style ! Line Drawing ! Outside !Double	44
Draw Single Lines Below Cells	Line Drawing	/Style ! Line Drawing ! Bottom !Single	44
Draw Single-Lined Boxes	Line Drawing	/Style ! Line Drawing ! Outside !Single	44
Edit a Cell	F2		5
Eject Page from Printer	Adjust Printer	/Print ! Adjust Printer ! Form Feed	121
Enable Undo Command	Undo	/Options !Other ! Undo !Enable	
Enter All Capital Letters	Caps Lock		49
Enter Data	Enter or highlight movement keys		6
Enter Formulas Without Typing	Arrow keys		15

Quattro Pro 2.0/ 3.0 Command Summary   **139**

Topic or Feature	Command or Reference	Menu	Page
Enter Sequential Values	Fill	/Edit !Fill	68
Erase a Block	Ctrl-E	/Edit !Erase Block	
Erase the Current Spreadsheet	Erase	/File !Erase	
Exit Preview Screen	Esc		127
Exit Quattro Pro	Ctrl-X	/File !Exit	23
Exit the Annotator	Annotator	/Graph ! Annotate,/,Q	101
Expose a Hidden Column	Hide Columns	/Style ! Hide Column ! Expose	113
Extract Part of a Spreadsheet, and Save to a New File	Xtract	/Tools !Xtract	
Extract Records	Extract	/Database ! Query !Extract	74
File Compression	SQZ	/File !Utilities !SQZ	
Footers	Print Layout	/Print !Layout ! Footer	119
Freeze Columns to the Left of Cell Selector	Locked Titles	/Window !Options ! Locked Titles ! Vertical	
Freeze Rows Above Cell Selector	Locked Titles	/Window !Options ! Locked Titles ! Horizontal	
Freeze Rows and Columns Above and to the Left	Locked Titles	/Window !Options ! Locked Titles !Both	
Frequency Analysis	Frequency	/Tools !Frequency	
Function Menu	Alt-F3		18
Go To a Specific Cell	F5		4
Graph a Block of Data Quickly	Mark the block, Ctrl-G	/Graph !Fast Graph	
Graph Title	Graph Text	/Graph !Text ! 1-2	89
Graph Type	Graph Type	/Graph ! Graph Type	78
Headers	Print Layout	/Print !Layout ! Header	118
Hide a Column	Hide Columns	/Style ! Hide Column ! Hide	113

140   Quattro Pro 2.0/3.0 Command Summary

Topic or Feature	Command or Reference	Menu	Page
Import File from Another Program	Import	/Tools ¦Import	
Insert a Column	Ctrl-I , C	/Edit ¦Insert ¦ Column	29
Insert a Graph into a Spreadsheet	Insert	/Graph ¦Insert	
Insert a Row	Ctrl-I , R	/Edit ¦Insert ¦ Row	28
Interior Labels	Customize Series	/Graph ¦ Customize Series ¦ Interior Labels	87
Interrupt Printing	Ctrl-Break		121
Leave Command Menu	Esc		8
Left-Align Text	Default		119
Link Cell Reference	[file name] cell address		110
Linking Cells	+, cell address		55
List Open Windows	Alt-O	/Window ¦Options ¦Pick	
Load a Linked Spreadsheet		Link Options	122
Load Quattro Pro	Q, from Quattro Pro subdirectory		
Loan Payments	@PMT		54
Locate Records	Locate	/Database ¦ Query ¦Locate	72
Manage Files with DOS-like Commands	File Manager	/File ¦Utilities ¦ File Manager	
Mark a Block of Cells (Extended Mode)	Shift-F7		40
Maximum Value	@MAX		52
Minimum Value	@MIN		52
Move a Block of Cells	Mark the block, Ctrl-M	/Edit ¦Move	41
Move a Cell	Ctrl-M	/Edit ¦Move	35
Move and Change the Size of Windows	Ctrl-R	/Window ¦Move/Size	
Move Between Windows	Alt-Window Number	/Window ¦Pick	109
Move Down One Screen	Pg Dn		4
Move Left One Screen	Ctrl-←		4
Move Right One Screen	Ctrl-→		4
Move Up One Screen	Pg Up		4

Quattro Pro 2.0/ 3.0 Command Summary **141**

Topic or Feature	Command or Reference	Menu	Page
Numeric Format	Ctrl-F	/Style ! Numeric Format	21
Open a New Spreadsheet	New	/File !New	26
Open an Existing Spreadsheet	Open	/File !Open	107
Open More Than One Spreadsheet	Open	/File !Open	118
Optimization	Optimization	/Tools !Advanced Math !Optimization	
Page Breaks	::	/Style ! Insert Break	118
Percentage Format	Ctrl-F, P	/Style ! Numeric Format ! Percentage	55
Pointer	..		18
Preview Graph	Graph Print	/Print ! Graph Print ! Destination ! Screen Preview	126
Preview Spreadsheet	Screen Preview	/Print ! Destination ! Screen Preview	119
Print a Block	Print	/Print ! Spreadsheet Print	46
Print Cell Formats and Formulas	Format	/Print !Format	
Print Date	@		119
Print Graph	Print	/Print ! Graph Print !Go	127
Print On As Few Pages As Possible (v. 3.0)	Print-To-Fit	/Print !Print to Fit	
Print Orientation	Graph Print	/Print ! Graph Print ! Orientation	127
Print Page Number	#		119
Protect Entire Spreadsheet	Options	/Options !Protection	
Quit a Menu	Esc		60
Quit a Menu	Quit	Quit on menu	50
Rearrange Text to Fit Specified Block	Reformat	/Tools !Reformat	
Regression	Regression	/Tools !Advanced Math !Regression	

142 Quattro Pro 2.0/3.0 Command Summary

Topic or Feature	Command or Reference	Menu	Page
Remove a Graph from a Spreadsheet	Hide	/Graph |Hide	
Remove Grid Lines	Grid Lines	/Graph	Overall |Grid	Clear	97
Remove Protection from/ Restore Protection to Cells	Protection	/Style |Protection	
Reset Column Width	Reset Width	/Style |Reset Width	
Reset Graph Settings	Graph Reset	/Graph	Customize Series	Reset |Graph	94
Reset Solve For Values	Reset	/Tools	Solve For	Reset	60
Retrieve a Spreadsheet	Retrieve	/File |Retrieve	94
Right-Align Text	¦ ¦		119
Run DOS Commands (v. 3.0 only)	DOS Shell	/File	Utilities	DOS Shell	
Run Quattro Pro from within Paradox 3.5	Paradox Access	/Database	Paradox Access	
Save a Graph	Graph Name	/Graph	Name	Create	84
Save a Modified Graph	Graph Name	/Graph	Name	Create	102
Save a Spreadsheet	Ctrl -S	/File |Save	9
Save a Spreadsheet with Another Name	Save As	/File |Save As	
Save a Spreadsheet after Changing It	Ctrl -S , R	/File	Save	Replace	35
Save All Open Files (v. 3.0 only)	Save All	/File |Save All	
Save Current Options Settings As Defaults	Update	/Options |Update	
Save/Restore Current Workspace Setup	Workspace	/File |Workspace	
Search and Replace Labels and Values	Search & Replace	/Edit	Search & Replace	
Select Command on Menu Bar	/, letter		8
Sensitivity Analysis	What-If	/Tools |What-If	

Quattro Pro 2.0/ 3.0 Command Summary **143**

Topic or Feature	Command or Reference	Menu	Page
Set Data Types for Data Entry	Data Entry	/Database !Data Entry	
Set Default Cell Formats	Formats	/Options !Formats	
Set Default Settings for Recalculation	Recalculation	/Options ! Recalculation	
Set Margins	Print Layout	/Print !Layout ! Margins	123
Set Up a Sort Key	Sort	/Database ! Sort !1st Key	70
Set Up a Block to Sort	Sort	/Database ! Sort !Block	70
Set Up a Criteria Table	Criteria Table	/Database ! Query ! Criteria Table	72
Set Up a Block to Query	Query	/Database ! Query !Block	73
Set Up a Block to Print	Print	/Print !Block	46
Set Up an Output Block	Output Block	/Database ! Query ! Output Block	73
Set Up Database Form for Data Entry	Restrict Input	/Database ! Restrict Input	
Set Up Graphics Printer	Graph Print	/Print ! Graph Print ! Destination ! Graphics	125
Set Widths of Columns in a Block	Block Widths	/Style !Block Widths	
Shade Parts of the Spreadsheet	Shading	/Style !Shading	
Solve for a Target Amount	Solve For	/Tools ! Solve For	58
Sort a Database	Sort	/Database ! Sort !Go	70
Stack Open Spreadsheet Windows	Stack	/Window !Stack	
Transpose Rows and Columns of Data Within a Block	Transpose	/Edit !Transpose	
Undo the Previous Command or Operation (If /Options !Other !Undo set to Enable)	Undo	/Edit !Undo	

144   Quattro Pro 2.0/3.0 Command Summary

Topic or Feature	Command or Reference	Menu	Page
Update Link References	Update Links	/Tools !Update Links	
Use Spreadsheet Titles As Headings	Print	/Print !Headings	124
View the Current Graph	F10	/Graph !View	81
What You See Is What You Get (v. 3.0)	WYSIWYG	/Options ! Display Mode ! WYSIWYG	
X-Axis Titles	Graph Text	/Graph !Text ! X-Axis Title	83
X-Axis Values	Series	/Graph !Series ! X-Series	80
Y-Axis Titles	Graph Text	/Graph !Text ! Y-Axis Title	83
Y-Axis Values	Series	/Graph !Series ! 1-6	80
Zoom In to a Window	Alt - F6	/Window !Zoom	108
Zoom In to Preview	+		120
Zoom Out from a Window	Alt - F6	/Window !Zoom	109
Zoom Out from Preview	−		120

Index

@

@COUNT, 52–53, 63
@IF, 61–63, 112–113
@MAX, 52–53, 63
@MIN, 52–53, 63
@PMT, 54, 59, 63
@SUM, 18–19, 24, 31–32

A

Absolute cell address, 16–17, 24
Add columns, 18–19, 24
Alignment
  center, 4, 67, 119, 128
  change, 51, 62
  left, 4, 6, 119, 129
  right, 4, 6, 119, 129
Alt-F3 keystroke, 18–19, 24, 31–32, 53
Alt-F6 keystroke, 112, 114, 116, 122
Alt-window number keystroke, 109, 116
Annotator, graph, 93, 97–103
Arithmetic, 6–7
Arrow keys, 2, 4, 6, 24
Arrows, draw, 100–101, 103
Ascending order, 70

B

Backslash key, 2, 7–8, 11, 98
Backspace key, 4. *See also* Corrections
Bar graph, 78, 81
Block
  copy, 39–40, 47
  delete, 46–47
  mark, 18–21, 24, 31
  move, 35–36, 41
  print, 46
Boxes, 42–45

C

Cancel command, 5, 8, 11, 41. *See also* Edit
Caps Lock key, 49, 63
Cell
  add, 24
  address, 4, 11, 16–17, 24
  align contents, 4, 6, 51, 62
  block, 19–20
  copy, 32–36
  defined, 3–4
  delete, 7, 11. *See also* Edit
  formula, 58–60
  linking, 55, 63, 111–112, 115
  move, 34–36
  reference, 106
  variable, 58–59
Centered text, 4, 119, 128. *See also* Alignment
Close command, 85–87, 90
Columns
  add, 18–19
  defined, 3–4
  delete, 30–31, 36
  fixed, 19
  headings, 123–125, 129
  hide, 113–116
  insert, 29–31, 36, 68
  width, 22–24
Comma format, 52, 63
Command Menu, 3, 7–8, 11
Command summary, 11, 24, 36, 47, 62–63, 75, 90–91, 103–104, 115–116, 128–129
Conditional statement, 61–63
Copy
  block, 39–40, 47
  cells, 32–36
  functions, 56–58
Corrections. *See* Edit

145

146 Index

Count items in block, 53, 63
Create
   database, 65–74
   graph, 77–80, 90
   spreadsheet, 13–23
Criteria Table, database, 72–73, 75
Ctrl-Break keystroke, 121, 128
Ctrl-A keystroke, 51, 62
Ctrl-C keystroke, 32, 36
Ctrl-Enter keystroke, 99–100
Ctrl-F keystroke, 21, 24, 51–53, 63
Ctrl-I keystroke, 28–31, 36, 68, 108
Ctrl-left arrow keystroke, 4, 11
Ctrl-M keystroke, 35–36, 41
Ctrl-right arrow keystroke, 4, 11
Ctrl-S keystroke, 2, 9–11, 23–24, 35–36, 106, 112
Ctrl-T keystroke, 107, 115
Ctrl-W keystroke, 22–24, 32, 52, 57, 63, 67, 111–112
Ctrl-X keystroke, 23–24
Currency format, 21–22, 24, 34, 52–53, 59, 111
Customize Series, 87, 94–96

D

Database
   copy formulas, 68
   criteria table, 72–73, 75
   currency format, 68
   design, 65–68
   extract records, 72–74
   field names, 69–70, 75
   fill block, 68–69
   locate record, 72–73
   menu, 70–75
   output block, 73–75
   query, 70–75
   search, 72–73
   sequential values, 68–69
   sort, 70–72, 75, 85
Date, print, 119, 129
Decimal places, 21
Default values, 94
Delete. *See also* Edit
   block, 46–47

   cell contents, 7, 11
   columns, 30–31, 36
   formula, 34
   key (Del), 7, 11
   lines and boxes, 45
   rows, 30–31, 36
Del. *See* Delete key
Descending order, 70
Display graph, 80–82, 84, 90, 107–109
Double lines, 42–45, 47
Draw
   area, graph annotator, 98
   arrows, 100–101
   lines, 42–45

E

Edit
   backspace key, 4
   block, 21
   boxes, 42–45
   cell, 5, 11, 16, 24
   column headings, 123–124, 129
   column width, 22–24, 32
   copy, 32–36, 39–40, 47
   delete, 11, 30–31, 36, 41, 45–47
   fill, 68–69, 75
   graphs, 82–83, 88–89
   Insert, 28–31, 36, 68
   labels, 5, 32–33, 88–89
   lines, 42–45
   mode, 5, 27
   move, 34–36, 41, 47
   page breaks, 117–118, 128
   series, 82
   values, 20–22, 27
Elements, graph annotator, 98
Ending cell, 19
Enter data, 6, 11
Enter key, 2–3, 6, 11
Enter-plus sign keystroke, 6
Enter sequential values, 68–69, 75
Escape key (ESC) 5, 63. *See also* Edit

Index **147**

ESC key. *See* Escape key
Exit
   annotator, 101–102
    Quattro Pro, 10–11, 23–24
    screen preview, 121, 128
Extended mode, 40–42, 47
Extract, record, 73–74
EXT. *See* Extended mode

F

F2 (Edit), 5, 11
F4 (Absolute cell addresses), 16–17, 24
F5 (Go to), 4, 11
F10 (View current graph), 80, 82
Field, 65–67, 70–71
File menu
  close, 85, 90
  exit, 10–11, 23–24
  open, 26–27, 36, 85, 107
  replace, 35–36, 47
  retrieve, 94, 122
  save, 9, 23–24, 36
Fill command, database, 68–69, 75
Footers, 118–119, 128
Formula
  cell, 58–60
  cell address, 6, 11
  copy, 33–34
  delete, 7, 34
  enter, 6–7, 15–16, 24
  quotation marks, 62
  subtotals, 31–32
Functions
  add column, 18–19, 24, 31–32
  conditional statement, 61–63
  copy, 56–58
  count items in block, 52, 63
  IF condition, 61–63
  links in, 112
  maximum value, 52–53, 63
  menu, 18–19, 24
  minimum value, 52–53, 63

  payment, 54, 63
  pointer, 19
  without typing, 19–20

G

Gallery, graph annotator, 99
Go command, 60
Go To key, 4, 11
Graph
  annotator, 93, 97–102
  arrows, 100–101, 103
  bar, 78, 81
  block, 80
  create, 77–78, 90
  customize, 87, 94–96
  display, 80–84, 90
  edit, 80, 88–89, 102
  interior labels, 87, 90
  layout settings, 125–126
  line, 86, 95–96
  menu, 78–80, 90, 95
  name, 84
  pie, 92–93
  preview, 126–129
  print, 125–129
  properties box, 100
  remove grid lines, 97
  reset, 94–97
  retrieve, 94
  rotated bar, 81
  save, 84, 90, 102–103
  screen preview, 119–120, 129
  series, 78–80, 82–83, 93
  split text, 99
  text, 82–83
  text box, 99–100, 103
  titles, 82–83, 89–90
  toolbox, 98–101
  type, 78, 81, 90, 92
  x-axis, 80, 83, 90
  y-axis, 80, 83, 90–91
Grid lines, 97, 103

148 Index

H

Headers, 118–119, 128
Headings, 123–125
Hide columns, 113–116
Home key, 5

I

Icons, graph annotator, 98
IF condition function, 61–63
Input line, 3–4, 6
Insert
    columns, 29–31, 36, 68
    page breaks, 117–118, 128
    rows, 28–29, 36
Interior Labels, graph, 87

K

Keyboard, 2
Key field, 65, 70

L

Label
    align, 4, 6
    apostrophe, 4, 50
    edit, 5, 32–33, 88–89
    graph interior, 87
Landscape orientation, graph, 126, 129
Layout, print, 118–119, 123, 125–129
Left-justified alignment, 4, 6, 119, 129.
    See also Alignment
Line Drawing, 42–45
Line graph, 86, 95–96
Linking
    cell references, 111–112, 115
    cells, 55, 63
    functions, 112
    options, 122
    spreadsheets, 105–115
Load Quattro Pro, 2–4, 11
Loan payments, 54, 59, 63
Locate, record, 72–73

M

Margins, setting, 123, 129
Mark block, 18–21, 24, 31
Maximum value, 52–53, 63
Menu
    bar, 8, 11
    command, 3, 7–8, 11
    close, 11
    edit, 5, 9, 28–32, 35, 41
    grid, 97
    pop-up, 10–11
    print, 46–47, 118–119, 128
    pull-down, 7
    quit, 63
    terminology, 8
Minimum value, 52–53, 63
Mouse, 131–132
Move
    between windows, 109, 116
    block, 39–41
    cell contents, 34–36
    one screen, 4, 11
    within windows, 108

N

NA. *See* Not available
Not available (NA), 122
Numbers, 33, 68–69
Numeric format
    commas, 51–52, 63
    currency, 21, 24
    decimals, 42
    percentage, 54–55, 63

O

Open command, 26–27, 36
Opening screen, 3
Open several spreadsheets, 107–109
Operations, arithmetic order of, 7
Orientation, graph, 126, 129
Output block, database, 73–75
Overwrite existing data, 74

Index **149**

P

Page breaks, 117–118, 128
Page Down key (PgDn), 2, 4, 11
Page number, print, 119, 129
Page Up key (PgUp), 2, 4, 11
Payment function, 54, 59, 63
Percentage format, 54–55, 63
PgDn. *See* Page Down key
PgUp. *See* Page Up key
Pie graph, 92–93
Plus sign key, 6, 11
Pointer, function, 19, 24
Pop-up menu, 10–11
Portrait orientation, graph, 126, 129
Preview graph, 126–129
Preview screen, 119–120, 129
Print
    block, 46–47
    date, 119, 129
    graph, 125–129
    headings, 124–125, 129
    layout, 118–119, 123, 128
    menu, 46–47, 118–119, 128
    orientation, 126, 129
    page number, 119, 129
    report, 121, 129
    screen preview, 119–120, 129
Printer, 121, 128–129
Properties box, graph, 100
Property sheet, graph annotator, 98
Pull-down menu, 7–8

Q

Q. *See* Quit command
Quarterly payment function, 54
Query, 70–72, 75
Quit command (Q), 10–11, 63
Quotation marks, formula, 62

R

Record, 65–67, 73–74
References, linking cell, 111–112, 115

Relative cell address, 16–17, 33–34, 62
Remove grid lines, 97, 103
Replace existing file, 35–36, 47, 112
Reset, graph, 94–97, 103
Reset values, 60, 63
Retrieve file, 94, 103
Retrieve linked spreadsheet, 122
Return key. *See* Enter key
Right-justified alignment, 4, 6, 119, 129.
    See also Alignment
Rotated bar graph, 81
Row, 3–4, 28–31

S

Save command, 2, 9–11, 23–24, 35–36, 102–103, 106
Screen preview, 119–120, 128–129
Search, database, 72–73
Select command, 8, 11
Self-test, 11–12, 24–25, 36–37, 48, 63–64, 75–76, 91, 103–104, 116, 129–130
Self-test answers, 133–135
Sequential values, database, 68–69
Series
    customize, 87
    defined, 78–80
    edit, 82
    menu, 79, 93
Shift-F7 keystroke, 40–42, 47
Shortcut keys
    alignment, 51, 62
    column width, 22–24
    copy, 32–34, 36
    edit mode, 5, 11
    exit Quattro Pro, 23–24
    extended mode, 40–42, 47
    format, 21, 24
    function menu, 18–19, 24
    go to, 4, 11
    graph display, 80
    insert, 28, 36, 68
    interrupt printing, 121, 128
    move between windows, 109, 116
    move, 35–36

150 Index

Shortcut keys *(continued)*
  save, 23–24, 36
  split text, 99–100
  windows, tile, 107, 115
  window zoom, 108–109, 116
Solve for menu, 58–61, 63
Sort, database, 70–72, 85
Split text, in graphs, 99–100
Spreadsheet
  close, 85–87, 90
  exit, 10–11, 23–24
  formula links, 109–111, 115
  hide columns, 113–116
  linking, 105–115
  margins, 123, 128
  open, 26–27, 36
  page breaks, 117–118, 128
  parts of, 1, 3–4
  print report, 121, 129
  retrieve linked, 122
  screen preview, 119–120, 129
  wide divided, 122, 128
  windows, 108–109, 115
Starting cell, 19
Starting Quattro Pro, 2–4, 11
Start value, 68
Status box, graph annotator, 99
Step value, 69
Stop value, 69
Style menu
  alignment, 4, 6, 51, 62, 67
  column width, 22–24, 32
  currency, 21–22, 24, 32
  hide column, 113–116
  insert break, 117–118, 128
  line drawing, 42–45, 47
  numeric format, 20–21, 24, 42, 51–52, 63
  percentage format, 54–55, 63
Subtotals, 31–32
Symbols
  apostrophe, 4, 50
  asterisks, 7, 21, 45
  brackets, 106
  colons, 118, 128
  parenthesis, 20, 24
  period, 19, 31
  pound sign, 119, 129
  vertical bar, 119, 128–129

T

Target value, 58–60
Text, 82–83, 99–100
Titles, graph, 82–83, 89–90
Toolbox, graph annotator, 98–101
Tools menu, 58–60, 63
Top heading, 124, 129
Type, graph, 78, 81

U

Underline, 44
Update refs, 122
Uppercase letters, 49, 63

V

Value
  change, 20–22, 27
  defined, 5–6
  start, 68
  step, 69
  stop, 69
  target, 58
Variable cell, 58–59

W, X, Y, Z

Windows, 107–109, 112, 114–116
X-axis, 78, 80, 83, 90
Y-axis, 78, 80, 83, 91
Zoom, window, 108–109, 116
Zoom box, screen preview, 120, 129